THIS WILL ALL BE OVER SOON

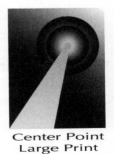

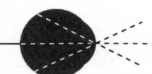

**This Large Print Book carries the
Seal of Approval of N.A.V.H.**

THIS WILL ALL BE OVER SOON

A Memoir

Cecily Strong

CENTER POINT LARGE PRINT
THORNDIKE, MAINE

For Owen and Leda—
my two favorite string beans
who remind me to listen for the birdsong
and look for the daffodils.

MARCH 24, 2020

I don't know how to tell this story.

I don't quite know what the story is.

Because I don't know when it starts. Or how it ends.

Maybe the story started with the awful day in January when I got the call I had imagined getting for almost two years but believed and hoped I'd never get.

"Owen has been given hours. His tumor didn't shrink enough where they could start the new treatment Monday. They will make sure he's in no pain, and he's surrounded by Ed and Laurel and Leda and his girlfriend, Stacia, and Sasha, his best friend since childhood. Soon he will go into a coma and then he will pass away."

I kept saying "No, no, no, no, no, no."

I don't know how long I sat frozen on my bed making these guttural wailing sounds. At some point I picked up my phone. I was in California. I was supposed to fly to Philadelphia the next day for a wedding. Owen was supposed to beat brain cancer.

That night, I took moments to glance at the clock on my phone, wondering, where in time and space was Owen? What part of his journey was he on at this particular moment? I suppose

I have my own magical thinking that began in earnest this night, that Owen would somehow beat this, too. I didn't know how. But if anyone could figure out how to beat time and space, it would be the smartest and most wonderful and bravest human I knew.

My little cousin Owen.

Maybe the story is a different story, and it starts at a Christmas party this past December with my friend Kevin. I'm a bit down, but we are having fun. At the very end of the night, I've had too many and my new agent comes over. I don't know what we even talk about, but he insists, "Just come meet the guy over there with the mustache."

The guy over there with the mustache is handsome. I almost say yes. But then I say no. I'm thirty-five. I'm very used to being single. The majority of my male friends are gay. The two men I'm with at the table are gay. I think it's sad that everyone wants to set me up, like it's sad to look at me or something. I'm doing great!

Okay, but I do like to smooch, and it's Christmas, and I feel cute in my outfit, so I talk to the man with the mustache. He's very cute. I have social anxiety, and I'm drunk and tired, so I have no idea what we talk about. He comes home with me. The next morning I'm a little more shy. He is less shy.

"Can I give you my number?" he asks.

I hand him the pink-flamingo pen my psychiatrist gave me that week. I find an old receipt, and he writes "Jack" and his phone number on the back. Now I have to text him first in order for him to have my number. I text him right after he leaves. I like him. Our timing isn't great. We both live in New York, but I'm about to go to California for a month. He's going to Cuba for two weeks. They don't have great internet.

Maybe the story starts March 2018. My dad has started a new thing I love, where he sends me a text almost immediately after each *SNL* show: a little summary that is, of course, always complimentary of his "girlie." This Saturday he doesn't text me. That's odd, but maybe he's just asleep.

The next morning he texts and says to call him. His tone immediately scares me: "I have some bad news about Owen."

Of all people, this is not who I expect. Owen is twenty-eight years old and in great shape, and what could be wrong with Owen?

"He was having migraines, and he took himself into the ER. He got an MRI, and they found a tumor."

We cried together on the phone. Brain cancer is a death sentence, right?

I went to see my cousins, Owen and Leda, at

my uncle Ed and aunt Laurel's apartment. I had no idea what to expect. What's it like after you find out you have brain cancer? I'm nervous on the way there. Owen's had surgery to remove the tumor. Will he be bald? Will he look sick? I am holding back tears in the elevator.

I get to the door and Owen opens it, his normal towering, skinny, string-bean frame greeting me, arms wide open for a hug.

"Hey, cuz."

I immediately feel okay. He's smiling. I hug Ed next, who is less confident than Owen. Then Laurel, who is always Aunt Laurel—determined and on some task or another. She seems busy. This is the first time I see it as an armor. She's going to make sure that we have snacks on the table and that everybody has water. She keeps the most beautiful home and always has— it's a magical skill to someone like me. My idea of cleaning a house is calling the junk removal people and shrugging like, "Have at it." Whenever I see someone subscribes to *Martha Stewart Living* I immediately know they come from a different monkey than I do.

Owen flops on a chair. Laurel is deaf in one ear, so he's always been used to talking loudly. I'm not sure what to talk about, but Owen leads the way. Soon I'm laughing. I love this kid so much: "You know how everybody goes online and goes on WebMD and panics and convinces themselves they have brain cancer? Well I'm the one who actually had brain cancer."

His doctors are great, he says. They've got a plan. He's got a plan. His only problem is boredom.

I hug him goodbye. I think I needed it more than him. Owen has this quality of being the one who supports everyone around him, even while being the one who is undergoing vigorous treatments for glioblastoma.

Uncle Ed walks me outside. He's visibly upset and nervous.

I say, "I think he's going to be okay. I really do."

And I really did.

Maybe the story starts Sunday, March 8, International Women's Day, when Jack comes with me to watch the US women's national soccer team play against Spain in the SheBelieves Cup.

He's excited to be at this big arena in New Jersey, to watch women's soccer with me. He gets choked up when he sees the number of little girls who get to have sports heroes, as it's still rare even though they are the most badass team in the world. But I digress. Jack is loving the game. US wins. Duh. Jack says he thinks women's sporting events might be his new thing. No loud, drunk guys.

We go out to eat and wait for traffic to die down before getting a Lyft home. As the restaurant starts to fill up, I wonder if this is a bad idea. The coronavirus is coming, isn't it? Although, I wonder, what is that really? I am more nervous than most people, so I shrug it off.

That night, Jack does this thing he does where he grabs my hands when I've absentmindedly started picking at the skin behind my nail. It's a thing I do. I pick at things in every way. It's nerves, it's anxiety. He notices.

He says, "I want you to feel like you can hold my hand instead."

I don't tell him, but it's one of the nicest things anyone has ever said to me.

We talk that night. Like, the talk I haven't had in six years. Are we dating? *I like you. Let's be dating.*

At first I thought it was so difficult to meet someone right as I was losing someone I loved so much. I knew he'd have to be patient with me. He'd have to let me grieve. It would be easier not to even try during that process. But grieving for Owen was like nothing I'd ever experienced, and I promised Owen and myself to continue to let all that love be there along with the sadness. So when Jack leaves that night, after the talk, I say, "I think you were a gift to me from Owen." And I like thinking of it that way.

Jack calls me that Friday morning and says, "I have a fever." Jack's got the coronavirus. What bad timing. So now you know how it could start.

Now it's time I tell you (if you couldn't already tell) I'm a bit lost. So here are some more parts of the story, in some order.

Owen tells me in August about a great new doctor he has, Dr. Henry Friedman. He's the head of neuro-oncology at Duke. He's leading the way in using polio therapy for GBM. That's the acronym for Owen's brain cancer. I'm learning the language of cancer now. Owen says Dr. Henry is the first doctor to bring up the word *cure*. I love this doctor. Owen starts polio treatments. I have no idea what that means or what it means for his body. In fact, I will never know what Owen experiences because he will never let on about the extent of his struggles. I'm not the only one. Doctors looking at his final MRI will say later that because of the size and position of his tumor, they didn't know how he was standing and laughing and talking as long as he was.

I'm in the middle of my two-week quarantine in my tiny apartment in New York. I've cried every day. I'm scared about Jack. I'm really scared. He has had a bad fever for a week. He didn't answer his phone yesterday. I text a doctor friend, who suggests a police welfare check. I end up not calling because I find Jack's roommate on Instagram and he responds to my message. He says Jack is just sleeping, but he's watching him just in case. This is how I meet Jack's roommate for the first time.

I have had anxiety and depression since high school. I take Wellbutrin. I've gone to therapy for years. I take Xanax when needed. This is a really bad time for mental health. Today I decide the anxiety is worse. I'd rather be depressed. I get really low. I wake up Friday and I turn my phone on airplane mode and I start drinking. I think it's going to fall apart with Jack now. I'm upset with him for not understanding why I constantly need to know he's okay. I'm upset with myself for needing to constantly know he's okay. I'm upset with friends talking about missing their fucking birthdays. What if Jack dies? What if I die? Owen just d—I can't say it or write it. I'm so low and I'm so afraid. I'm afraid of the water coming out of my pipes. I'm afraid of outside. And I am so alone. I've never felt so alone. I ask Owen out loud to please help Jack. To help me. I immediately feel bad for asking. I just feel bad.

The next morning Leda texts me that she's upstate. She says she's heard a lot of birdsong, so we are in good hands. Thank you, Leda. Thank you, Owen. Perfect timing.

Maybe it starts on January 18, at Owen's memorial service, when I spoke about the weird little red-haired boy I first met as a kid who came back into my life as an adult and taught me about

14

family and what it is to feel that kind of love. I talked about his love for birds. The boy who loved birds flew away.

I send Jack the video of Owen's beautiful service. He is still feeling sick, but his fever has finally broken after ten days or so. He tells me he went to high school with one of Owen's friends, Nate. Nate from Antarctica!

"Nate's coming from Antarctica. Can you believe it?" Laurel said as she went through letters and emails and flowers in a much quieter apartment, days after Owen had gone. We ate dinner, and I tried to make them laugh a little. I think Owen would want that. I know he would want that.

Jack's roommate sends me a video after Jack's chest X-ray and doctor visit. Jack is in a mask and gloves. He's out of breath. He's tired. He looks sick. He says the X-ray looks good. He coughs. Then, even though he's out of breath and sick, he still says, "My doctor is such a great doctor." I rewatch this video in my quarantine. It makes me laugh a little. It makes me cry. He's really sick.

Leda told a story at Owen's service. She had asked one of Owen's doctors if he was scared when she told him they couldn't do anything more for him, that he would have hours to live. I had this thought, too. But I knew he wouldn't be scared. The doctor said that while most patients panic and try to bargain in this moment, which makes me really sad to hear, Owen didn't. Instead he thanked her for trying her best. And for all she'd done for him.

So I don't know what this story is. The world is upside down. I'm holding devastation and love in equal measures. What is bad timing when the timeline seems irrelevant? What's the ending? Would you even know?

MARCH 26, 2020

Matt and Kevin are going to pick me up at six thirty. It's five now and I've just dropped a bag full of tiny clamshells and shredded lettuce all over my kitchen floor. I don't even have time to take a theatrical moment and laugh about it. I clean quickly. I've got to get everything out. I'm leaving this apartment and New York City for five weeks.

I'm hoping I've thought of everything but I don't quite trust my own head right now. I've packed as well as I can after what has felt like two weeks of a hurricane inside my brain. The only human face I've seen is my sweet dog walker, Carlos, who pokes his head in twice daily to get my eight-year-old rescue dog, Lucy, for walks. They say it's safe to walk your dog as long as you maintain six feet. But I don't risk it. Nothing feels safe out there.

Actually, there is another human face I've seen. Earlier this month, Owen's doctor from Duke, Henry Friedman, reached out—because his patients become family, and he had not met Cousin Cecily yet, but also to ask if I'd be open to maybe mentoring a young actress whose family he is very close to. I said of course, although Syd, this young actress, was already a Broadway star in her own right, so I wasn't sure what I could

17

do. I made tentative plans to have lunch with Syd and her mom, Keri. And then about a day later, New York shut down. Then Jack tested positive for COVID and I started my quarantine.

So instead of meeting Syd and Keri for lunch, I wound up frantically speaking with Keri over the phone about holistic methods for treating respiratory illness, like liposomal vitamin C and manuka honey. She had a lot of experience with taking care of a close family member who had suffered a couple of bouts of pretty serious pneumonia. But I wasn't able to buy the honey or vitamin C because other people clearly had gotten the same advice and there was none available online or from any store that might deliver in New York. Keri said she could spare some of hers. So she and our teenage Broadway star phenom Syd drove all the way from somewhere *not* close to give sick Jack in Brooklyn and maybe-sick me in Manhattan each a box of liposomal vitamin C. They also gave us each a roll of toilet paper, because it turned out nobody was able to get toilet paper. I watched Syd through my peephole, smiling even though she couldn't see me, as she left my little COVID care package outside of my door with a cute note before running back down to her mom waiting in the car. We didn't have much information yet by then, but I knew I wasn't allowed to open the door.

I ask my doorman if he will send the big cart up in the elevator to my floor. I never got rubber gloves so I'm wearing a black glove from a curling wand I bought recently and holding a scarf from the dog groomer. I awkwardly load up the cart with the weird things I've chosen to bring. A salad spinner. A nice salad bowl. My garlic press. A yoga mat. Vodka. You can't get things on Amazon right now.

I have trouble maneuvering the cart in the elevator but Lucy is already in there. My mind flashes quickly to that story about the dog leash getting caught when the door closes and the dog being hanged. I'm panicking again. Stop. No time. I'm almost in a splits position to make sure the door stays open as I get this damn cart in. I'M GETTING OUT.

The street feels scary when I'm out there. I hope they pull up soon. The virus is out here. I glance at my doorman, Mervin, and I feel guilty that he has to stay. I hope he stays safe. I hope he knows he and Carlos are superheroes.

The boys pull up and we try to figure out how to get everything in the car as quickly as possible. Finally I whip off my coat and get Lucy on it. Seat belts on and we hit the empty streets. It takes a couple minutes before we say hi and acknowledge that we haven't really seen people for two weeks. And we all sort of fake-laugh about that and get quiet again. I'm with

19

my friends Matt and Kevin. We've been friends for seven or eight years. They are coming to an Airbnb in the Hudson Valley with me for the next five weeks. They say we are still weeks from the worst of it in the city.

"Can we listen to the Cranberries now?"

I texted the boys earlier today, asking if we could listen to "Dreams." I like that song and I like singing in cars. We all sing together. It feels good. We decide to listen to more Cranberries. We do the hits. The sun is setting and I take my phone out and take a video. I've never been a good photographer, or the one who takes the pictures, but I want to right now. Because I'm so happy to be outside. Not happy. I'm not happy really. I don't know what I am. I am not in my apartment anymore. I am 90 percent less scared. Tonight anyway.

"Ode to My Family" comes on. We all sing along. I know almost every word. I remember in fifth grade, my friends Erica and Susannah and I all recorded ourselves doing very serious music videos to this song. Solo. We each got our own video. Same sad song, though. My idea. What a fun kid.

We reach the end of the song—"Does anyone care? Doo doo doo doo doo doo doo doo"—and I see Kevin bobbing and swaying his head *so* hard. We are really going for it with the doo doos. And I start giggling. Then I start to really laugh. This is insane. We are, like, dancing hard to the doo doo part of this sad Cranberries song on our way out of New York City because coronavirus is now seemingly everywhere in the city and Kevin and I work on shows that have all been postponed indefinitely and Matt's office is closed and there isn't time to question the fact that your whole life just changed also indefinitely and what will happen and what does any of it mean who cares DOO DOO DOO DOO and suddenly they are laughing so hard too. And finally we are all laughing really hard.

Matt says he hasn't laughed for real for almost two weeks. Kevin says, "Me too." I know they aren't lying. I laughed for the first time a day ago. We have all been fake-laughing and nervous-laughing, so you feel the difference when it's real.

I was on the phone with my agent yesterday. I was still laughing a little from an *SNL* group text exchange that had me in tears earlier. I work with really funny people. My agent is in LA. I think they are starting to feel how we felt two weeks ago. The virus is making its way over, it seems, and the nerves and sense of unease are taking the same journey. Although, let's face it, nobody does anxiety like New York!

My agent said, "Glad to hear you are going to write and you are laughing." And I said, "No no no, you don't understand. I'm not *going* to write.

I'm just *hoping* to write. And now I feel like I've got a shot." And what he didn't understand about the laugh is that I was laughing but it was the laughter of a person who has just popped their head above the water and said, "Ha! I survived the shipwreck! Whoopee!"

The rest of the car ride, we keep laughing. It feels good. We aren't even laughing at super-funny things. Somehow SlimFast comes up and I put on that stupid soft nineties accent and say, "It's easy. I have a shake for breakfast, a shake for lunch, and a reasonable dinner." We are cracking up. "It's *sensible* dinner." We are dying laughing. It's become a running joke. *I have a "____" for breakfast, "____" for lunch, and a sensible dinner.* Insert anything. It's funny to us still.

Matt cries a little after he really laughs in the car. It's weird and it's not a new concept: "Laughter is the best medicine." But now it's not just a cliché. Now I'm feeling it in real time. I'm seeing what a real laugh can do. I'm seeing how often we force the fake laughs and I know why we do.

MARCH 27, 2020

This is what I wrote and got up and said at Owen's memorial service:

The Strongs are a bit of a WASPy bunch, which to me meant my immediate and extended family was a small fraction of the size of my Catholic friends' families. Although Owen and Leda are technically half Jewish and half Episcopalian. A combo which, Owen informed me, made him "Epissy-Jew." There are two Strong branches in our immediate family: the New York Strongs and the Chicago Strongs. Well, my dad says New York Strongs. I call them the String Bean Strongs, as they are long and lean like string beans. While the Chicago Strongs are just a little less "long."

While age differences are a much bigger deal as kids and can keep you from getting close, I loved getting to visit my "little" cousins. I was so enchanted by this funny little boy with bright red hair who could be so ridiculously serious at times. And then by his somehow equally-wonderfully-bizarre-in-the-best-way little sister, Leda. My grandma Scotty would laugh as she told me some new funny story about them. Like the time Owen confronted some New York construction guys who were working in his apartment, storming in saying, "I'm three years old and I'm not afraid of you." Or when Leda, who had a bit of a low voice as a toddler, told a waitress, "You have very nice blood circulation."

The thing I knew most about Owen as a kid, though, was that he LOVED birds. Like to an obsessive, comedic degree. Because also, what kid chooses birds?!? One time, Owen put together a beautiful bird model and while tossing it around the Tolsons' backyard to see it fly, the dog got ahold of it and wouldn't give it back. This resulted in lots of tears, but also lots of laughs as a distraught but very determined five-year-old chased a little dog around all afternoon to save his beloved bird. As an adult, even Owen conceded his love of birds was pretty funny, and why the hell didn't he study ornithology? He couldn't tell ya.

He was full of surprises. One time in the park when Owen was chasing pigeons instead of playing on the swing set (naturally), we asked what he would do if he caught one. Knowing Owen, you'd think it would be to maybe keep it as a pet. Or study it. Or play with it. His answer was: "I'm going to catch it and fry it in butter." And then he grinned.

When I came to New York for my first couple rounds of auditions for *Saturday Night Live* in summer 2012, Owen made sure to see me every night. Even though I had only seen him once or twice in over ten years. But he showed up, and we had a blast every time. He even sang some Shaggy at karaoke with my friends and me. And over the past seven or eight years that showing up never stopped. I think finally by around the third year I stopped being so surprised to see all or some of the New York/String Bean Strongs at an event that I hadn't even bothered inviting people to, knowing how busy life is in New York especially. But Owen kept showing up. Usually with Leda in tow. No questions.

And I realized I was starting to feel that I was never without the support of my family. I don't know many people who possess their selflessness and kindness. So I tried to tell my cousins as much as possible how proud they make me and that I'm forever awed by the amazing people those silly little kids became.

25

And speaking of, I'm so grateful I finally got to meet Stacia. The girl who changed his life. The girl who would text him she was on her way home and he'd respond "Hooray!" every time. And that level of happiness is usually only reserved for our dogs when we get home. So much rarer in humans. What a gift to know he was so puppy-level happy after finding this great love with you. In the midst of what may seem like a tornado to all but the bravest and most special people.

I told Owen often that he was my hero. And he was. And even though I hate even bringing up his cancer, I do so because during the last year and a half, Owen somehow took on the role of OUR fearless leader. Showing all of us how to fight. How to smile. How to stay full of love. How to "take no guff," like he told Stacia before work every morning. How to throw a massive blowout balls-to-the-wall badass thirtieth birthday party. Let the world do as it may. That's a real-life hero.

So how to make some kind of sense of any of this, and the pain now filling so many lives that it seems our tears flooded the streets of New York earlier this week. How to somehow wave goodbye to the little boy brave enough to stare down giant construction workers. Brave enough to chase a wild dog for hours to save his bird. Brave enough to show up anywhere ever for anyone. Brave enough to sing karaoke in front of strangers and share his own music with the world. Brave enough to hit any dance floor. The man brave enough to fight a cruel and unpredictable disease and never let it take his spirit. Brave enough to fall madly in love in the midst of it all. I don't know how really. So today, all I can think to say is that it seems the brave little boy who loved the birds so much flew away before the rest of us.

After the service, a friend of his from college came up to me. I was holding a roll of toilet paper. (It must say something about the way we were raised that my brother and I separately showed up with our own rolls of toilet paper to use as tissues.) There were so many different people crowded in this theater in New York, really speaking to what kind of a person he is. I realize I'm using the present-tense *is* as opposed to the past-tense *was,* and it's because Owen's presence in all of our lives feels like a thing that will continue to be, and probably evolve, and not something that has ended. And I know that's a thing I think everyone says after a funeral: that the number and different types of people in attendance are a testimony to the person being honored. But I don't say it as a loving but sort of generic memorial to him. The room (theater actually!) was packed. Young and old. Family and friends. My friends were there. Leda's friends. Ed's friends. But the room wasn't that way because those people wanted to support us. The room was that way because Owen was really friends with all of us. He liked his uncle as much as he liked his college buddies. He enjoyed hanging with his dad's cousin. He liked my friends. Your friends became his friends. He once texted my friend Mackenzie after a surgery to ask how she was doing. The kid with brain cancer checking up on my friend. So that's why that room was so special. He made all of us feel like a friend and welcome anytime.

Anyway, his friend from college told me that he thought Owen would have really liked what I said. And that he was really thankful it was funny. Now, I didn't try to write something very funny. But I felt so low and I tried to still follow Owen's lead and not be too sad about him even though initially I thought I was doing that to help him stay strong and beat it. But I made that promise, and so it still doesn't feel right to break it. And I still won't give cancer the win. It never beat Owen because it never got his spirit. So I wrote something I hope made people smile and laugh once or twice. And I tried hard not to cry too much when I read it.

Okay, but back to his friend. He said he had held it together really well during the whole service because it was all so sad. So he was able to be stoic. But then suddenly he laughed and then he finally wept for his friend. And I think Owen would be okay with that, don't you? He laughed, too, after all.

MARCH 28, 2020

A really cool thing happened yesterday at my safe house retreat in the Hudson Valley. I'm slowly easing my way back onto social media, sort of. I have a message from re—inc. It's a clothing company founded by some of my heroes on the US women's national soccer team. It's about making gender-neutral clothing and sizes, and also they are women soccer players, and I don't know if you've heard, but there is a bit of an equal-pay problem happening there, so I am supportive of all their other ventures.

They sent me a message asking how I was doing in New York and if they could send me something to cheer me up. It was really nice. It chokes me up. Now that I'm out of my scary apartment and scary New York City, I am finally able to feel other things. My tears are happy again. My laughs aren't forced. The kindness of people reaching out to New Yorkers makes me happy-cry. I tell them. I tell them I brought a re—inc shirt with me, stuffed into the bag of all the clothes I'd had to choose for these five weeks. I brought it because it makes me happy. I'm writing to them while wearing my soccer hoodie. I tell them all of this. They write back that it brightens their day, and would I like to do an Instagram Live thing with Megan Rapinoe via however that works? I say, "Of course! Wow!" I tell Matt and Kevin. They say, "We'll do hair and makeup!" I say, "No, you won't. I'll do hair and makeup. You'll help with however the fuck you do an Instagram Live with another person somewhere else."

I love Megan Rapinoe. When the women's World Cup was going on, my friend Rashida, who I call my little sister, and my friend Nnamdi, who used to play pro soccer in England, and I never missed a game. We all got jerseys. Rashida wore 13 for Alex Morgan. Nnamdi wore 17 for Tobin Heath, who is a beast on the field and also happened to have the same number Nnamdi wore when he played. I wore 15. Rapinoe. My kind of American hero. She stands up for what she believes in and it never feels shallow. She was the first white athlete to kneel during the anthem. The whole team was suing their bosses for equal pay while playing, and dominating, in the World Cup. The president rage-tweeted at her (well, actually, he rage-tweeted at a K-pop teen fan with a different spelling of *Rapinoe,* because of course), and two days later she scored the first goal against England to help the US win a big match. And she stood arms outstretched, smiling proudly. It was the anniversary of Stonewall. It was nice to be able to say, "This is also what an American hero looks like."

31

When the team came back to the US for the victory tour, they played their first match in Pasadena. I felt so lucky because I was in LA. I made sure Nnamdi, Rashida, and my friend Bianca (another big soccer fan and favorite human) were there. We got to sit in a box even though I was worried there was no way I would be able to score those seats in LA. Wouldn't everyone want to be there?? I mean, AMERICA JUST WON THE WORLD CUP! Sure, it's the women's World Cup, but come on!! I guess women's sports still have a ways to go, but whatever, this is a celebration! And there was still a huge crowd. And there were celebrities there. Rashida wasn't wearing her glasses. She pointed toward the next box over from us: "I *need* that jersey." I looked where I saw a man standing with his back to us in a "BURRELL 19" jersey. "You *need* a Ty Burrell jersey?" The man was Ty Burrell. "Oh. I just saw the four stars."

Then we saw the back of a man's head walking with his daughters to the field. Who was that? He was far away. He must have been important though, because he was walking onto the field, taking pictures with the team. I said, "I think that's Kobe Bryant." Later, as he made his way back up to his seats, we confirmed. It was definitely Kobe Bryant.

A week after Owen's service, a helicopter in California went down carrying Kobe and his daughter Gianna. It was heartbreaking. The nation was mourning. Leda and her friend Erika and I had made plans to go to the Knicks game earlier that week. We still go. I can't wait to see her, to give her a hug. There is a big picture of Kobe outside of Madison Square Garden. I take a picture. I don't know why. I don't want to be like a tourist at the Colosseum, but fuck it, it just feels like this is a strange time. Important to save. Isn't this a way to capture a moment? For what, I don't quite know.

We are inside. Leda pulls me aside. We hug. She's been so strong. I want the world for her. Once we get inside the Garden, she nervously asks, "What do you think about waiting to go to the floor until a little after the game starts?"

"Why?" I ask. She knows basketball *really* well. She's going to Columbia for a master's degree in sports management.

She says, "Because they will take a moment for Kobe."

And immediately I know what she means. I'll do whatever she wants. We wait a minute. Not a minute. Less. We decide we want to be there. We want to mourn and celebrate Kobe. With the crowd.

We are on the floor. The whistle blows and the players stand still. The Jumbotron shows a great big beautiful picture of a smiling Kobe. The crowd is silent, and then they start to cheer.

They cheer for this guy they loved. The guy who brought his daughters to that soccer game. Everyone is shouting, "KOBE! KOBE! KOBE!" And everyone is in this together. I turn to Leda and I start saying, "OWEN! OWEN! OWEN!" And she smiles and she says it with me and we are crying and yelling his name.

MARCH 29, 2020

I've decided the next thing I want to do is the most personal. I want to share my text messages with Owen and Leda with you, to let you know them a little more. My memory is sometimes faulty, and I really want you to know the level of specific kindness and love I was fortunate enough to share then, and share now.

I go to my phone and my thumb freezes, hovering above the button to search *Owen*. It's raining today. And tomorrow, turns out. Kevin, Matt, and I are all in separate rooms. I haven't heard from Jack today. I don't know what's happening with us. It's a dark day. So I'll wait until tomorrow to share those texts, I think.

That night, Dr. Henry calls. He makes me feel better. He says that's part of his job. He asks me to look up a video I made for Owen right after his initial diagnosis. I asked my lovely castmates to record videos cheering Owen on in his fight. This was at the beginning. I remember I wasn't sure I was supposed to call it brain cancer at the time. Was it? My castmate said *brain cancer* at one point in the video and I remember wondering if that was okay. Should I edit? Was that in fact what Owen had? It's not like I was going to call him and ask to clear that point up. Actually, writing that now, it makes me laugh, because he would have explained it to me without a second thought or thinking it a weird question. Probably would have explained while eating something, talking through bites.

I find this text, and I want to share with Dr. Henry:

Owen: *Hey Cec! Thanks for getting my back! Love you too! Yeah Henry (he won't let us call him dr Friedman haha) is the best. Looking forward to this new treatment*

And right after, I send Dr. Henry my own message: *You are the best, Henry. Thank you.*

MARCH 30, 2020

So I think I'm gonna get the hardest out of the way, the one that kept me from doing this yesterday. But it's important, maybe. Maybe not. But I need to get it out of the way.

Tuesday, January 7 9:18 PM

Cecily: I love love love you and while I'm not worried about you because you are the strongest person I know, I mean that, I'm beyond sorry you have to go through any of it. I'm behind you 100% rooting for you and shouting for you. Let me know if there's anything cool I can send to you or do for you ♥.

That is the last text I sent him on a phone I don't know if Owen looked at again. I learned later he had been readmitted to the hospital after the doctors called that morning, saying he needed to be rushed in after looking at his MRI from the previous day. He would leave us "officially" on Saturday, early early morning. Sometimes I feel sick or guilty. Did I take it too lightly? I didn't. But I did believe there must still be a way. Part of me is happy I didn't say goodbye to a boy who didn't tell us he was going. Who am I to make that choice for him?

Leda was in Peru that week. Had just gone on vacation. She had to fly home immediately. But she got to the hospital and she got to be with him. So here is the second-hardest text:

Friday, January 10 6:08 PM

Cecily: I'm sorry to text now. But please let him know how much I love him and how much he means to me

Saturday, January 11 5:07 AM

Leda: I love you

So much

Okay. Those are the hard ones. Now, the reason I felt like I could write this today was because I found one of my favorites last night after looking up videos for Dr. Henry.

I wore a special shirt at good night in March 2018. (That's the part of the show at the very end where the cast, host, and musical guest all come together on the main stage—"home base"—as ourselves to say good night to one another and the audience. This is usually the first time during the week I'll speak to the musical guest, a fact that disappoints at least half of the people who ask me about the show.) John Mulaney was hosting. Owen was still very recently diagnosed. I was still recently allowing myself to say *brain cancer.* The shirt, which I made, said "G'Owen Strong." Then I got this text:

March 18, 2018 10:27 AM

Owen: Cecily . . . the t shirt. Oh man. Seeing you wear that at the end of the show warmed my heart more than you could know. You are truly an amazing person who ALWAYS puts others and the problems of the world she is passionate about before herself, and not in the easy passive way, in the active way that demands real sacrifice. You are obviously extremely talented and smart and funny and beautiful. You're the best cousin ever and I love you

I will hold those words with me forever. I miss him right now.

Okay, and now for something funny, the parts of the story I like to live in. Big brother, little sister, older cousin talking basketball. Little sister *loves* basketball. And basketball player:

39

November 8, 2018

Leda: Are you allowed to DM basketball players if it's — — — and he makes your story his story?

Owen: No

Stop

Please

Cecily: I mean, yes. But also remember it's — — — who is liking a story that's praising him. And that maaaaybe doesn't happen a lot? So, as long as you keep context in mind :)

Leda: Hahaha

All valid points

Owen: I didn't make a point

Just want you to stop

Leda: I think "no" is a point

Just not a nuanced one

Owen: Haha fair

Leda: But yes Cecily I'm great at keeping context in mind

November 5, 2018

Owen: In the hypothetical situation that the New York Knicks run into the stands and tag you in, and you have a wide opportunity to score on the bulls, your former home team, would you do it? Would you dunk on the bulls?

Cecily: Absolutely. The way they treated Derrick Rose?!?

If Michael Jordan was there no way

But also

I can't dunk

I can hardly jump

I can barely walk

Owen: Psh well not with that attitude you can't

Leda: I in fact can dunk

And would happily do so

If tagged in for the New York Knicks

Owen: That's the spirit

Cecily: Then I'll pass the ball to you

Guys I don't want to NOT dunk on the Bulls!

I tried never to prod too much about Owen's GBM, instead letting him decide what and when he wanted to share with me.

March 12, 2019 2:46 PM

Owen: Hey Cec! Just thought I'd give you a quick update on ma brain sitch. Just finished my second MRI review appt today in Carolina and the treatment is working excep-tionally well. The tumor is rapidly disintegrating. Obviously no guaran-tees but if I continue like they expect me to and like people in the past who have responded like I have thus far then I'll be sticking around a whiiiiile longer. Basically the news is as best as it could possibly be. I just wanna thank you for all the AMAZING support you've given me thus far. I mean the friggin video, the friggin T-shirt on stage, your usual amazing loving self and words, you are truly the best cousin I could ask for and I love you so much. Fam chill sesh/ dinner soon!

Cecily: Wow ok this is the best news I could hear. I'm a dweeb and you got me crying this morning! I am beyond inspired by you my dude. More than you could ever know. And it's gonna stick with me a long time. I'm of course so sorry you've had to deal with any and all of this. And I'm happy to be in your corner and I'm thrilled I get to call you family because you are one of the toughest and smartest and funniest and kindest people I know! Thanks for sharing this update. I'm with Rashida now and I'm gonna share with her if that's OK.

Owen: It's crazy. I'm insanely lucky.

MARCH 31, 2020

It's still raining. I got this text from Leda after sending her some of what I was writing:

> Leda: I can't believe you just sent this now because I was literally sitting among the daffodils that just bloomed at my country house and thinking of O. My mom planted daffodils when he was born and his birthday is always right around when they bloom. And then I came back just now and read this. And I'm crying again of course. I love what you said about finally writing about Owen now because the world needs cheering up, and maybe it will make people more happy than sad. I was just talking to my therapist about how I struggle to share stuff on Instagram bc I want to celebrate him so bad but don't want to look like I'm asking for attention.

> Cecily: I think you can journal. And I think you get to celebrate him as much as possible. Everyone who

knows you and knows Owen would love to see you celebrate him.

Leda: My dad for the first time the other day apparently learned the phrase "don't cry because it's over - smile because it happened"

Cecily: FIRST TIME?!? HE WORKS ON BROADWAY

Leda: But it's been really helping him. I didn't want to take anything away.

It's harder to feel good right away, turns out. Even in a beautiful house outside of a city that scares you. I'm glad to write about Owen. To relive these moments.

APRIL 1, 2020

Jack is healing and getting better and better every day. He is still in Brooklyn with his roommate, taking the time he needs there. It hasn't been easy on us. I wonder if I'll lose him. I really hope not. I want it to work out, and I'm going to try, but unfortunately it seems I have very little control over what happens in the future. Especially in an upside-down world. Today it's raining. Tomorrow and the rest of the week it will rain. Corona will continue to get worse across the country and globe. But I've had a lot of sunny days. And who knows what happens next week. They say the curve will flatten eventually.

Yesterday Leda posted a picture of herself in the country kneeling with the daffodils. It's a simple post.

"I love daffodils."

She's getting there. I'm getting there.

APRIL 2, 2020

I'm so tired. This week I've slept a lot. My faithful Lucy next to me. Depression is exhausting. Exhaustion is exhausting.

Last year, Leda posted a picture on her Instagram for my birthday. It was the three of us. It was taken the summer of 2014. I was planning on going to Hawaii to shoot some scenes for a movie. But those plans had just changed. Instead, I found out I was secretly going to Boston to shoot some scenes for *Ghostbusters*. I couldn't do both. But friends had thrown me a going-away party anyway. Even though I wasn't really going anywhere yet. And when I was, it was pretty close. Owen and Leda were at the party. Because they always were there. Anywhere. Easily sitting among my friends. Big smiles.

Owen had a scruffy look that night. His hair was a bit longer, and he had some scattered longish auburn facial hair. Later on, he became much more clean-cut. Not stiff though, by any means. He was still laid-back. He reminded me of a Kennedy. Not only because of his looks (both he and Leda are very beautiful), but because of his manners and grace and elegance and ease around formality and drunken going-away parties alike. It's something I've never learned. I'm the one who showed up to the service with the toilet paper roll in my giant overstuffed purse.

My dad and his older brother, Ed, were military brats. They grew up all over. My dad was born in Germany. Ed wanted to name him Gerhardt. My grandma and grandpa chose William. Bill. Billy to his mom. Or Billy Boo. My grandma was called Scotty, because of her Scottish background and the fact that my entire family was very fond of nicknames forever and ever until our generation. My grandfather was Colonel Cecil Strong. My dad had to answer the phone "Colonel Strong's residence. William speaking." Cecil had a friend named Colonel Poopy Conners. I love that name, which is the only reason I'm including it. Ed was better at the discipline part of being an army brat than my dad, I think. One of the stories I managed to get out of my dad was that in grade school once (in Turkey, I think) his teacher told him his book had dog ears. And he turned and told her she had dog ears. But he wasn't all sass, because when Cecil was stationed in Georgia, and the family lived there, my dad's report card featured a glowing note from his teacher, who said, "Billy is a fine southern gentleman."

Cecil passed away of a sudden heart attack at the age of fifty-seven. Ed was in college. My dad was seventeen. That's why I can only manage to get some stories out of my dad. He's locked a lot of it up. It's painful. I've only seen my dad cry a handful of times. Mostly recently, because of losing Owen. Once with my brother and me in front of Cecil and Scotty's graves at Arlington National Cemetery, the only time I've ever visited with him. But other than that, he's been a bit of a closed book, and it's okay. I keep trying. I found pictures on Ancestry.com once of Cecil and his many brothers in college. I saw a yearbook photo of his brother Howard, my great-uncle. I showed my dad and said, "Wow, he looks like Owen."

"He does, a little bit, yeah. Pretty sure he was gay."

I texted the photo to Owen and Leda, too. I liked texting them what I could remember about our grandma. Scotty developed Alzheimer's pretty young, in her late sixties, I think (although it's hard to pinpoint when it started, which is normal for that heartbreaking disease), and she passed away in 2006 when I was twenty-two. The year feels a bit irrelevant, though, as it felt like I had lost my wonderful, lively grandmother already by the time I was in high school. I adored her. She had a fun Southern accent (she was from San Antonio, Texas) and Jackie O hair. She always wore turtlenecks and scarves and coral lipstick. She loved to laugh. She dove for a Nerf football once while visiting and had to get stitches. She called me Lulu and would tell me when she had to "wee wee." She told me stories about her brother, Pooh (Alan), and her sister, Jessie. I would sit on her lap at my dining room table and make her tell and retell. I liked talking to Owen and Leda about her, who never got to really know her like I did. They were younger than I was and she got sick pretty young even though she "lived" to be eighty-one. I told them the stories I could remember.

While I got to know Scotty very well before we lost her, or what was really her, my dad and his brother, Ed—Leda and Owen's dad—had a lot of military friends of the family and extended family members who I never really got to know. But Owen and Leda seemed to know all of these people somehow! Like, they were having brunch with them! I had no idea who any of them were, nor even could I imagine how to behave in the presence of disciplined military folks. I went to art school and love the F-word and hardly know the rules for ordering a pizza over the phone. But Owen fit in well with everyone, everywhere.

And again, it was never fake with him. The smiles were real for everyone. He just maneuvered between worlds really seamlessly. He could work in the corporate world of the Dursts (Aunt Laurel's family) and then go on to write and perform music with his band the Evening Fools.

I always do this. I get lost trying to tell one simple story. I told you I was lost.

• • •

When Leda posted the picture of the three of us at the party, as I said, it was 2019. February. Owen was more clean-cut by then. She wrote, "Remember when Owen Strong looked like this?" And he wrote, "Thanks for making me look like I time travelled, Leda."

And now here I am, Owen. Time traveling. Looking for you.

APRIL 3, 2020

His birthday is coming up. In two days.

I didn't go to his party last year. And I remember the guilt I've been holding deep in me in that place you hold the things you can't reach so you can never clean it out.

It was a big one.

Thirty.

He had a big party as strangely diverse in its attendees as his service.

My dad showed me a video on his iPhone and I laughed when I watched because my dad accidentally filmed some lady's back for ten seconds because he was clearly having difficulties with his eyesight, working his iPhone, and wanting to watch the action in person.

A very "dad" video of an important event.

But it's all I had.

Because I wasn't there.

I couldn't go because of work.

I'm sorry to miss it, I told him, not lying.

But I did miss it.

And now I can't work.

And he won't have a party this year.

APRIL 4, 2020

When I spoke at his service, I spoke with my dad. I figured we could hold each other up. At one point I noticed he was grabbing two pages instead of one and was going to turn two pages and miss a page, so I tried to slyly help him, so he could keep saying the words I knew were as important to him as mine were to me. With no moment of confusion trying to find his place. It's another way you can lean on one another. I also didn't want him to feel "old" or embarrassed. He, of course, being the fast-thinking and deft public relations pro he has always been, turned it on me by slightly chuckling and thanking me and then making some joke about cue cards on *SNL*. I don't know. Not a great joke. But, pride or whatever, you know. Maybe I needed to lean on him more than he needed me.

We talked a bit before about what we would be saying, how we didn't want to overlap. For instance, we both wanted to share the same story from an old picture I had of four kids in a hotel pool. It's me, two other kids who were family friends, and Owen. The three of us other kids are all around eleven. Owen must be about six. He had just broken his arm. He had a bag around his cast and he was walking around the shallow end of the pool all day and asking over and over, "Does anyone think this is fun?" It's one of my favorite stories. He was such an oddball. But in this particular picture, none of us are smiling except for Owen, who is *grinning*. No one smiling except for the kid with the broken arm in the pool.

My dad said he wanted to speak for my uncle Ed. And he just kept saying, "Why? Why Owen? Why now?" There is no answer of course, and I wasn't so sure I loved asking it right then because it felt angry, and again, I wanted to try my best to keep my grief as full of love as possible, as I'd inwardly promised myself and Owen, wherever he was.

I've occasionally thought that maybe we were lucky to have lost Owen when we did, that awful day in January, instead of now. But I never really could say it. Because to say that makes you think you are somehow "putting it into the universe" that you feel lucky that someone went and really you'd rather they hadn't even had brain cancer in the first place! But here we are, almost three months into having lost him, and we are lucky he went then because of what we wouldn't get now. We were lucky because he got to be with loved ones in the hospital, singing with them and holding hands and hugging. We were lucky because we got to have that service and we got to hug each other. I was hugged the longest by an older man I don't know, still don't know, but

we held each other for such a long ti
saying how sorry he was.

Maybe I can offer up one answer
question: why Owen?

Owen fell madly in love after being diagnosed. He released two of my favorite songs with his band. One amazingly right before his last week in the hospital. He helped arrange the strings on that song, without even being able to play any strings. He went to basketball games. He covered scars with hats and became the fun guy who collected hats. He came to *SNL*. He danced. He smiled. He laughed. He read. He ate ice cream. He told my uncle he'd had the best year of his life.

The entire world will be affected in some way by coronavirus. We don't know how. We don't know if we will be sick or someone we love will be sick. Could the unthinkable happen and could we actually lose someone? And why can't we control this fucking thing? I watch Cuomo speak to try to understand the science. We try to wrap our minds around the language of COVID-19 and Ebola drugs and malaria drugs and what it does to your body, and we can only watch, helpless.

I hear and feel the fear and pain and grief and sadness in people and how it manifests in lashing out and hoarding and turning on one another, and it's dangerous and it's sad and every day I have started to feel it more and more: the world needs Owen Strong.

sounds hyperbolic and, quite frankly, ossible, I realize. I don't mind the hyperbole, nce I still see him as a bit of a superhero figure. But I guess what I really mean is this: I was afraid to talk too much or share too much of this loss for many reasons. It would mean acknowledging something as real when I wasn't ready to, I wasn't sure it was my loss to share, and I was afraid of never being a good enough writer to properly honor him, just to list off a few.

Now I'm ready. Leda is ready. I want to write about him. I want to talk about him. I want you to know him. I want you to feel a little better after knowing a bit of his story. Maybe, just maybe, somebody will feel less afraid about the uncertainty that lies ahead. Maybe we can find moments during a very scary and difficult time to feel lucky.

Because who knows: as Owen proved, the worst year of your life could turn out to be the best year of your life.

Maybe that's why, Dad.

APRIL 5, 2020

I'm adjusting to life in the Hudson Valley with Matt and Kevin. I almost erase that sentence immediately. Or put quotes around *adjusting*. I feel like every sentence I've written lately I've wanted to qualify, explain how the words aren't quite right for what I'm feeling. But maybe I just have to accept it's because nothing is feeling quite right and every word feels too "soft" and I don't feel like going too "heavy" is very helpful for me right now.

I am slow to adopt FaceTime and the Zoom— whatever people are doing. Jack (who is still in Brooklyn and still in my story, which makes me happy) thinks it would be good for me. To combat loneliness and missing people. But it's not being alone that is making me feel lonely. And I'm just not ready for all my friendships to turn into bad views of my face, when I'm also someone who likes to be able to look away when I need to. And for me, phone calls "just to chat" always feel so forced or something. I've always found them a bit rude. The timing always seems better for one person. I don't mind the idea of interacting without being in person. I love to text. I love to write emails. I think it offers more space for people to take their time to respond when it's convenient, and you can really think about what you want to say. Phone calls for me have always been for emergencies and business. Not friendship chats. Because it's never been like what it's like when I'm with my friends in person. Where all of a sudden you may get up and dance. You can laugh. You aren't going, "What else, what else." Pauses don't mean anything. Silence is acceptable. You aren't just "updating," you are creating and discovering, and I'm using words that sound important but in my head I'm applying them to even the silliest and dumbest situations and conversations and games, I promise. It feels alive and like anything could happen. I love that.

I was thinking about things I miss in that vein the other day. I miss the possibilities for small adventures. (I am rife with anxiety so will never be a "big adventure" person.) Or at least it feels like my window for small adventures has narrowed tremendously. I am going to use the following word incorrectly and it's probably culturally insensitive, and I'm very sorry if so, but I also know I am using it incorrectly and think of it as a separate idea in my head but certainly lightly connected to what I lightly know about the origins, and I don't have another word yet and it's a great word and it's in fact my favorite way to describe what I mean here: I love a walkabout. (Remember the Chili Peppers song "I think I'll go on a walkabout / Find out what it's all about"?) I like the idea of setting out with no map and no plans and no schedule. Following what seems like where you want to go. I like the idea of just starting a night out walking and seeing where you end up.

This led to my somehow becoming an almost regular at an open mic near my apartment a few years back. Not as a performer. As an audience member. I've seen friends ride mechanical bulls. Been to a secret after-hours flamenco bar run by "La Doña," who had to approve of you before you were invited back. I like being with my bizarre friends in California and having a wig drawer and inviting them over and just seeing what happens. Maybe you end up performing your own new Peter Pan musical with improvised music and lyrics and choreography. Or maybe it could lead to going out to a Christmas party you aren't sure about because you aren't feeling so hot and meeting a nice man with a mustache.

I like conversations to feel this way. I like surprises. I like being surprised by others. I like surprising myself. I love waking up in the morning and saying, "That was the craziest night ever," while I'm still laughing. I love when you wind up just dancing for hours, so sweaty but unable to stop. I love when you wind up meeting someone new and you talk and maybe cry with them for hours. I love all of the possibilities. A phone conversation isn't bad, it just feels less alive. Maybe I'll just have to find the ways I can do it in this new normal.

But also I don't know where I am yet. I don't want to resent friends who seem too "happy" or feel like I'm supposed to be in a certain place. So I'm just avoiding till I feel a bit better. It was only two weeks ago, to the day, that my phone was on airplane mode and I lay in bed drinking, wishing to find a way to stay sleeping for longer because being awake meant feeling so so low. That's not really the person I want to share.

I don't know. I'm sure my thoughts on all of this will change. Because they'll have to. Because I miss people. But I also know the disappointment of a desperate quick fix can hurt, and I'm trying to avoid those things.

While I say all of this about missing people, though, I'm burying the lede, which is this warm text relationship I'm developing with my Airbnb host, Megan, whose name I might have to change later if I ever share this journal or book or whatever it is with anybody, because of her safety. The town has become increasingly hostile about people from the city coming up to the Hudson Valley and spreading the virus. Or buying all their toilet paper and all that bullshit. I've tried to be very respectful and careful about all of this coming in. It's felt very hurtful. It's made me preemptively defensive. Anyway, I don't want to spend energy there. So I won't.

Megan has been a shining light. Every day she offers up some new comfort. She offers to extend my stay again if we need. She's sorry about what's happening in New York. She lets me know if we get bored, she has more board games at her other home. She tells me she'll drop off a third bicycle next week. She will ask her partner where the pump is so we can all go riding. And they'll load up and clean the kayaks for us anytime, and we can follow them to the river, where they will leave them for us, since they have the rig. She sends me a picture of the river in spring. It is actually gorgeous. I don't know how to kayak. But then I think, *I guess there's no better time to learn a solo sport than when you've got nothing but time and you must be solo.* She says not to worry, there are life jackets. I thank her every day. She thanks me. She opened a restaurant this year and now they can only deliver and do curbside pickup and they have to close at eight. We are helping each other, Megan and I. I like her and I decide to open up and let her know her beautiful home has also provided me an opportunity to finally process a lot of grief I hadn't yet about losing my young cousin in January. She texts back saying she lost a family member to brain cancer.

I have found in the last two months that I know a lot of people who have lost someone to brain cancer.

This morning I wake up to a picture of the board games. *Just let me know if any of these interest you and we can drop them off this weekend.*

So I guess I have made a surprise friend and am having a sort of little adventure after all.

Oh, and I waved to the UPS man from the window in the kitchen yesterday. He waved back.

APRIL 6, 2020

I found out Matt shares his birthday with Owen. He bought a cake. We are ordering from the one other restaurant that delivers right now. It's Mexican. I'm sure it's not great. But it will be great no matter what, you know? We'll have margaritas. We will dance. We'll have a three-person-one-dog party.

I've been playing music and I say, "I want to play just one more song and I want it to be just the perfect song for us for right now." I scroll through my Apple Music library on my phone. I don't want something too sad or too happy or slow or fast. I take this job seriously. It takes me a long time.

I find the song.

Just a perfect day
Drink sangria in the park

I'm singing along while leaning on the kitchen island.

I smile at them.

"This is the right song, right?"

So proud of myself.

"What is this? It's amazing."

"You don't know 'Perfect Day'?? By Lou Reed??"

How do they not know this song?

We listen to the whole thing. They love it. It's the perfect song. I found the perfect song.

Earlier in the day I felt bad. And then it's as if from somewhere in the birdsong, Owen said, "Don't feel bad, cuz. Look! You're having a birthday party! In a quarantine!" Maybe it's a coincidence. But that's not really important or relevant. In a time of feeling like we don't know anything anymore, I know I feel like I got a hug; I was reassured. By a person who was so good at reassuring.

Thank you, Owen. Happy birthday.

APRIL 7, 2020

Today is the first day I question whether I can do this.

I was sitting in the sun. And I looked at my phone. We were laughing at the new nickname I'd come up with for Lucy. Lucia Maserati Donatella Versace. And then I looked on Facebook.

Oh my God.

Hal died.

Of COVID.

Hal Willner. Longtime music producer on *SNL*. My friend and the coolest of everyone I work with on the show.

I stand frozen, looking out at the trees and the pond, and the boys walk quietly inside. I start to cry. I check to make sure this is real. I text my good friend Erin at the show.

Hal died.

I know. I just heard.

And I'm stuck again. Stuck standing.

I want to say goodbye in a panic because it feels like people don't get goodbyes when thousands die at once and people are unique and strange and some of them are the most bizarre members of your workplace. They deserve a goodbye we are not numbers we are not numbers we are not numbers.

He took a liking to me when I first started. I thought it strange but I liked it. I gladly accepted it.

Then I remember. He and I just emailed. He was setting up a concert for Planned Parenthood over this hiatus—which was supposed to last two weeks in March, but now it's a bit unclear when we will actually return and I don't know what other word to use—and asked if I would like to perform or intro someone. I couldn't because I was going to LA. Then I wrote back: "I canceled my trip because I'm paranoid that I touch my face too often and it's not worth the risk to fly so I can do the show." He had to cancel the show anyway. The musicians didn't want to fly in. He ends the email: "Withmuchlovetoyou, h."

We are losing people to corona that we've talked to about corona.

I'm reminded immediately of a line Tom Davis wrote in one of my favorite essays, "The Dark Side of Death." I look it up. Davis was one of the original *SNL* writers. He helped create memorable characters like Nick the Lounge Singer and the Coneheads. He wrote this essay after he was diagnosed with cancer. He wanted to go on his terms. He declined chemo and stayed in his house in the Hudson Valley.

That makes me hold my breath.

I find the line.

"Ironically, I will probably outlive one or two

people to whom I've already said goodbye."

Today I find it very hard to write because today I find it very hard not to be angry. I started getting angry last night. I'm angry at friends who don't see that there are one hundred thousand more cases in New York and want to talk about themselves or class issues or anything else. Or who pretend "it's sad everywhere." I want to scream, "NO IT ISN'T! IT'S NOT LIKE THIS! HAL DIED BECAUSE WE ARE FIGHTING YOUR STATE FOR GOODS AND SUPPLIES AND YOU DIDN'T BELIEVE ME WHEN I SAID JACK WAS SICK AND YOU THINK A TEST IS A VACCINE BECAUSE YOU DON'T READ THE ARTICLES ALL DAY BECAUSE YOU DON'T NEED THE SCIENCE TO LIVE."

And the whole point is to not be mad, right? I don't like that side of me. I want to shut off from people. I resent my loved ones. I feel like a dog snarling in a corner in a shelter, and you feel bad because you know that dog will never be adopted like that and if only she was adopted she would be given the love and care she needs, the lack of which is making her lash out in this shelter.

But I think there will be more days like this to come, and maybe I'll have to accept being mad, too. And I will remember I am here and I'm getting this chance to write and hopefully share Owen.

Today it feels like I can't do it. So maybe this is all I can write for today.

Hal never quite felt "of this earth." Now he is no longer on this earth. I hope you are floating in a magical outer space of music, Hal.

Fuck COVID.

APRIL 8, 2020

Do you know how pathetic it feels to be hurt by boy drama when the sky is falling?

But here I am.

I haven't eaten in two days. It's that diet when someone is starving you of their affection. I'm a corona meme now. A girl talking about boys and food.

I've tried so hard to stay on top of this. To rise above of what I knew this would feel like. And to make it not real because it feels like some freak accident.

I'm not allowed to text Jack because he told me the other day he wanted a break from me. This weekend he was planning to come up to visit me for a week. He told me he won't be doing that now, it wasn't a good idea. Everything was too much for him. I have no choice but to leave him alone, even though it hurts so much. I can't be mad like I normally would, the mad that protects you from being too sad, because he just had a pretty big health scare. The rules are different.

So instead I open up a new file in my notes in my phone. Here's what I've written:

The things I want to text: I miss you. I hope you aren't gone. Time has moved so slowly but I'd give anything to go back to have a good night and hold your hand again. Right now I want to bite my fingers off because they serve as reminders.

It's hard not talking to you or getting geeky pictures. I can't let myself look through geeky pictures. I hope you are thinking of me.

Remember when we texted pictures of our doctors at Weill Cornell?

I almost got to see you. I almost got to touch you.

I'd give the world to come to that warehouse-looking building in Gowanus.

I wonder if you wear your sweatshirt.

I wonder if you kept your painting.

I want to go to the Berkshires.

You sound like Bob from *Bob's Burgers*.

I hope someday I get to show this list to you.

What happened?

Can't it just be normal again?

I miss my dear Jack so much.

Do you know how much I like you?

I'm so sorry I ever made you feel so bad you walked away.

I wonder if it will keep me awake every night.

I wonder if I'll get to talk to you and how fucked up it will be if that doesn't happen.

What happened?

I liked being on a team with you.

I know I have jealousy issues and all that bullshit and I also know it sucks and I want to get rid of it and I think it takes a person like you. I wish you could see I see my shit as "gross" too, but it's real. And I wish you could see I don't want it. Maybe is there a world where we let ourselves be imperfect humans?

I know I'm always questioning myself. I question you, but I really don't want to. I want you to help me be normal. I want me to help you be whatever it is that you want that you think I have any power to help move along. And I want to live our lives and get to know all of you more along the way. And let you keep melting me.

I want to know what I do that hurts you this much.

I want to know when (if ever) I'm allowed to talk to you again that it will go better. It's all I want.

I want to know why you left.

Or maybe not. Maybe it's better I don't. If it's not helpful.

But I want to know you'll find a way back to the weird and wonderful first little pig's home we made. And it was blown down. I'll build it back up myself the

71

minute you let me. I was following the advice of my beloved cousin's doctor— and that's why I thought it was okay also to check up on you and ask your doctor. I didn't know it bothered you as much as it did. Can you believe that sad irony? I really thought maybe you were feeling supported knowing we were there for you. I thought your parents liked me then. I wanted to do what I could. I'm sorry I got it wrong. I'm sorry it felt oppressive. If I knew it would lead to losing you, I wouldn't have ever ever ever said a thing.

I know you can't respond to this. I know I shouldn't send it probably, but I lost a favorite person and friend and I'm trying to be respectful and figure this out. You don't have to read or respond. Of course I'll accept crumbs right now, but I'd rather the whole loaf of bread later on.

I'm sorry while you were sick I was sick in a way that made it worse for you. It makes me feel terrible. And even with all the heavy talk, I miss just any talk. I miss flirting. I'm very smitten. I'm gonna work on the hardest thing ever which is patience and the blank spaces in relationships because you are very worth it in a very human way (you aren't perfect).

I'm sorry that I may send an email sometimes. It's very hard to be in isolation and lose my favorite voice. But want to respect it. I hope you aren't angry about this. But I suppose I understand if you are. I can't control a thing!

I made chilaquiles. I forgot to tell you I make those too.

APRIL 9, 2020

I did the Instagram Live thing with Megan Rapinoe yesterday. It was supposed to be a talk about renewing and resetting and what is draining to me and how I work around that. We'd had a great conversation the day before on another new videoconference app I had to learn. I had sort of prepared what I would say. Sort of.

Then an hour later I heard about Hal.

I emailed them that night and let them know the situation, but I said I was still open to doing the Live because, like with this writing, I am trying to be honest and present and open so I can best deal with all of this and not bury my head in the sand, the depressed ostrich. And I know I am one of many grieving any number of things right now, and maybe it's good to put a face to that too. Because I don't know if people know they are allowed to grieve. I don't know if people even *know* they are grieving. Or scared. Or anxious. And the re—inc group had been so kind to me. They reached out to me. Early on. Which was so touching because I felt so alone and that bit of kindness meant so much. Megan emailed me separately last night and promised to take care of me. I knew I would be safe.

And selfishly I think I did it because I wanted

the connection, too. I am a solitary person but had work and friends and travel before all this. I could stay in really well because I went out really well. But I can't do that now and I'm lonely and I think this is how I can feel less alone. I don't want to talk to a friend I may sort of resent or feel too different from right now. I don't want a long conversation with my parents. I'm just not there. I don't know why. Maybe it's because I don't want anything where I have to force a smile. I don't want to bother with social niceties if I don't have to. If it's not waving to the UPS man or texting Megan, our Airbnb host. I prefer writing to the anonymous "you" reading these words. I prefer talking to Owen, who is somewhere in time and space and the birdsong. I want to be comforted by my favorite athletes in the world over email and Instagram Live. What a bizarre time.

I also felt last night that there is a phenomenon right now where although so much feels frozen and slow, it turns out your grieving must be quick. I felt a panic to say goodbye, to honor Hal. Because Hal died Tuesday night.

And in New York City, he was one of seven hundred.

And I was just one person mourning Hal. Among probably thousands—all the people who worked with him on *SNL* for all those years or any number of the crazy, wacky, amazing, and sometimes unbelievable artistic and musical endeavors he was part of, including the album of pirate songs he produced featuring Tom Waits and Patti Smith. It's like he knew everybody.

And it's not good between Jack and me. Our different experiences and reactions—the sick one and the one afraid for the sick one, and now the one who has recovered and so is less nervous about COVID and the one who has to remain afraid. And through all of it only getting some long phone calls, some brief ones, and some texts. It feels so unfair. And I know that sounds crazy to say *that* feels unfair in the midst of everything else going on. But I guess I feel okay saying it because everything else just feels devastating and way beyond just "unfair." This is unfair. Not to get to see someone, not to have them hold your hand so you stop picking at your fingers. To have this kind of stress put on something I got to really enjoy for the first time in so long, something I was looking forward to at the "end of this." I had dreams about how good that hug would feel.

But who knows. Who fucking knows anything.

I talked to Kevin yesterday and said if this were "real life" I'd be panicking and calling Jack and crying hysterically and it would feel a bit like life or death to save it. But I don't have that luxury. Ha.

How to grieve in isolation? Magical thinking, some delusions, stories . . . therapy, of course therapy. I have a wonderful therapist I speak with over the phone now. She had COVID in March.

But nothing heavy. Because if I let anything become too heavy I won't make it. I won't be able to write. I won't be able to make myself come for what we're calling "family dinner" each night. I won't be able to walk outside when it's sunny. I won't be able to find moments to feel lucky.

I have to learn to adapt to this new quiet solitude sitting in the eye of a terrifying devastating tornado. I have to learn how to connect and I think I'm getting better at it here, now, than I ever have been, somehow. I have to learn to grieve better. I have to learn patience, which is insanely tough coming from eight years on a weekly live sketch show where everything we do is fast. I have to let myself cry when I don't want to because I know crying leads to laughing too.

There are so many memes online—the whole world is online now—of people showing a cat crying or something and it says "ME." And I told Kevin last night that it's just like the forced laughter. Everyone feels so weird, and I think half of people think they are "supposed" to be either crying or laughing so they just put out this little picture to sort of lightly do both.

And while I appreciate the effort at solidarity or wanting to express some kind of emotion, I want to say, "No, thank you. I'm not a cat." Neither, I realize, am I that snarling shelter dog I compared myself to recently. I'm a person, and I'm crying because I lost my amazing cousin Owen in January and I was really scared and depressed and panicked for two weeks in my apartment and really lonely and the person I really liked was in an unknown danger and I didn't know what would happen to him and now I might have lost him anyway and one of the kindest and strangest and coolest people I know died of COVID Tuesday night. And I'm just one person and I don't say any of this thinking I have it "worse." I just want to say it. I just want to tell you my story.

And then I want you to tell your story.

APRIL 10, 2020

Today I went through the old texts, curious. Just when was that show? He had just recently been diagnosed. He hadn't met Dr. Henry and Duke and polio treatments yet. He was starting radiation but nobody quite knew what that meant. What did that mean?

It was March 2018.

> Leda: Just saw that the April 7 show is Chadwick boseman and Cardi b . . . any way I could go to that show? I'll watch from a coat closet. That's my future husband thooo.
>
> Cecily: Of course!
>
> Leda: Omg amazing ♥♥♥ you are my hero And that's the day after Owen's bday! I can see if he'd feel up to coming.
>
> Me: YES!!!! If he wants to do the earlier dress version of the show at 8 instead I'll see what I can do. And I'll try to get floor seats.

> Leda: I have faith that Chad will fall in love with you and hope he does so that I can meet him and try not to cry and maybe get a pic I'll frame forever.

Leda and even Owen are always lightly hinting that they'd like to see some love in my life, in the way only your polite little cousins can. I tell her of course she can come.

> Leda: Amazing!!! I'll talk to him now but he might not know a little closer to then. They said he won't even feel side effects of radiation until 3 weeks in so he might feel totally great!

> Me: Ok wonderful. I'd flip to have you there. And I can try to have you meet people! We can do the party and the whole thing.

> Leda: Yay! I'll talk to Owen and get back to you.

She does exactly that.

> Leda: I was talking to Owen about the April 7 show and he was thinking dress rehearsal might be better. Would it be ok if the two of us went

to that but then I stayed for the actual show in the dressing room? And then the party? And then someone will have to kick me out eventually . . .

They get there that night for the dress rehearsal show. My wonderful colleagues have taped off great seats right up front. Reserved for them. They helped me give them the VIP treatment.

Leda: Ok well we didn't specify we were the cuzzes so now we're just in line. Can we just tell the next person we talk to? I mean if they're taped off for us they won't give them to anyone else right? At least not right away.

Me: Oh no of course not They are yours! VIP bb.

Leda: Owen and I want updates on your date after.

Cheeky cousins. I had a good first date recently and I guess somehow I slipped and told my little cousins about it, and I can only think it was from seeing them right after the diagnosis and being nervous still and thinking I needed to talk to fill space, and so I guess I offered up my embarrassing dating life. Of course my cousins don't treat it that way and only want to give me pep talks. Oh, and that guy and I had a very mediocre second date.

Owen is tired, but sure enough he's there in some nice coat, tall and skinny and handsome and smiling and right there and thrilled to walk around a bit after the show. My castmates Alex and Chris take pictures with us on the stage. I love them so much for this I can't tell you. I'm worried now about time as it's between shows and we are on the set and I have our pre-air show company meeting in Lorne's office soon. And I wonder if Owen is embarrassed by taking too many pictures anyway, like I am. I wonder if he is tired. Or *how* tired, I guess. So we get four pictures. Then I move us along.

All the pictures are so dark. You can hardly see us. I'm wearing leopard-print slippers and leggings next to gorgeous Leda in a sleek black midriff-baring suit and Owen, standing center, like a distinguished tree, his arms over and around the whole group. I wish I would've taken more time to make sure the pictures were good. But part of me is glad I didn't. It's okay to not know what to do. It's okay to not treat every moment like it's maybe the last, and if it were, would I want to spend the time getting a good iPhone picture?

He went home not long after the photo. Leda stayed at the show, and although I didn't go to the after-party after all, she went with her friend Shanda. They tried to get pictures with Chadwick but he said he was too tired.

Today I smile because I remember the sketch I wrote with James, Kent, and Kate that week for Chadwick. It's a sketch about sort of nerdy traveling a cappella singers. And it's so funny to me right now because it hits me—*duh!*

Owen sang in an a cappella group in college. In fact, that was my second-to-last text on my message thread with him. At one point around Halloween last year I was talking to someone who surprised me by saying he was into a cappella groups, so I texted Owen.

> Me: Hey what was your a cappella group called at school?
>
> Owen: S Factor. Why? Is *SNL* looking for a musical guest? Ha ha.
>
> Me: Ha ha. No I was talking to an a cappella freak and I brought you up and he asked the name.

It didn't occur to me until now. It's like we wrote that sketch just for Owen!

APRIL 11, 2020

There was a little thunderstorm today. I don't like when it rains. We have a "gale" warning till Saturday. There was an alarm wailing outside for some time this morning. It felt too heavy, too sad. Because it sounded too much like sobbing, heavy weeping and moaning. Lucy was scared and ran under the bed.

But now the sun is out. I'm sitting up, writing. Lucy is next to me on the bed.

I'm lucky.

APRIL 12, 2020

It's Easter. Have I said that in twenty years?

Last night I did another Instagram Live. I'm trying to "get out" more. I talked to Jack on the phone for the first time since he told me he wanted the break. It was nice, I think. I can't do this without some sort of delusion, some sort of magic.

I talked to my friend Whitney today about all of it. I sent her some of what I've been writing and she read it and she's crying. We talked about the importance of making room for magic in our grieving.

So here is a magic story for you:

Saturday Night Live aired last night, an "at home" special. I wasn't really there. I haven't been here much this week. I'm trying to come back, but I'm not ready. I want to laugh. I know the importance of laughing. I want to make people laugh. But I'm just not there yet.

The producers are very gentle with me about this, especially my good friend Erin. She's wonderful and we've been close since my first year. It was her wedding I missed in January. I actually asked Rashida to text her. I had no idea what I'd text. It seemed absurd. *I'm sorry I can't come to your wedding tomorrow. My cousin just passed away. Will you be able to fill my spot? I hope you don't lose money. I hope I'll stop crying someday.* I'd say "passed away" or "passed," something like that. I don't know if I'll ever be okay saying the word *died*. Erin has suffered some big losses in her own family. She sends flowers to Owen's service. She comes, along with her husband and her baby daughter. She tells me she remembers how seeing a baby at her father's funeral service was so important to all of them. There is something hopeful about it, or at least distracting in a really good way. I think she is wonderful.

She understands I can't do the show yet. We do a Zoom table read on Wednesday or Thursday and everyone is a face on a square on a screen now and we're seeing each other but not really and we can't hug each other and we are all in shock I think because of Hal. I'm doing it from my bed. We silently wave goodbye to each other at the end. It's as much as I will contribute to this first episode. It feels so wrong and somehow disrespectful to my grief to go on TV, however we do it, and I pretend that I'm okay. I'm not okay. But I promise Erin I will be. I want to be okay again. I will get there. She knows.

I watch that first episode with the rest of the viewers live that night, not knowing what this show will look like. It feels strange. They do a really nice special tribute to Hal. Because we haven't shown up at work, hearing his voice and seeing him makes his passing that much more surreal. I hardly remember what anyone said. I was crying throughout, Kevin with his arm around my shoulders.

Because during the Hal tribute, they play one song. They sing along to the song.

The song I sang and danced along to on the night of Owen's birthday.

Just a few nights ago.

The night it turns out Hal was leaving us.

It's "Perfect Day" by Lou Reed.

I cry harder.

APRIL 14, 2020

I heard something once that's always stuck with me, about why we get the pins-and-needles feeling in our hands and feet when blood flow has been restricted and then comes back. Because the blood is bringing that body part back to life. And coming back to life hurts.

It's our fourth week in the Hudson Valley. It feels like it's been no time because of how little has changed or moved, and it feels like such a drastically different world that years may as well have passed.

I had a good talk with Jack today. And it was good because I am finally in a place where I can say the rules have changed for me. How can we be the same as we were over six weeks ago? How can you date someone the way you want to? But I don't think you can go through isolation by just cutting someone off. I didn't like feeling hated or shunned or something. And I'm not. That was important to hear. I needed that. He is dealing with his own coming back to life, and I am dealing with mine. And someday maybe we will be in the same city, and we can see each other, and maybe we will want to smooch again. But for now, I am content with a voice on the phone who I can have a good conversation with. That's actually really nice.

The rules have changed.

Life has changed.

It most likely will change again.

Not a dramatic change. Not huge. Not in ways I can know how to describe yet. I feel like I should be sadder than I am. At the same time, I feel sadder than I should be about something vague and distant that I can't put my finger on.

I do believe that it doesn't have to stay sad. It doesn't have to stay painful. The blood comes back, and it hurts for a bit, but then it's okay. Things change. It will be different.

New York has been without Owen since January. *SNL* will be without Hal, if and when we come back. We will come back. I will work again. I made a video today. I'm doing Instagram Lives. I'm adjusting. I'm not fighting. It's not what I prefer, sure, but it's what I've got, and I will hopefully find a way back to the person I like best.

Maybe not, but it's what I choose to believe. You can choose to believe brain cancer is a death sentence. Or you can believe in polio therapy. Dr. Henry believes it. Owen believed it.

That's the team I want to be on.

I'm not where I want, but I'm where I am, and I am choosing to try my best to not fight any of it and instead discover my new rules.

1) Nothing too heavy.
2) Notice the sunshine.

3) It's okay to cry as much as it's okay to laugh.
4) Say yes to these Instagram Live shows more often.
5) Do your makeup if you want. Feel pretty.
6) Don't feel bad for wanting to feel pretty.
7) Trust yourself just enough to know that although you think the idea that everything happens for a reason is bullshit, you do think you are doing this the best way you know how, and you should be proud.
8) It hurts to come back to life, but all of this has made it hurt less.

Four weeks have passed since I started writing.

In my solitude you haunt me
With reveries of days gone by

That Billie Holiday song just popped into my head.
I miss so much.

APRIL 17, 2020

Do you also cry yourself to sleep?
  So often?
  I keep approaching "okay."
  But I'm never fully there.
  I'll only ever be "okay adjacent."
  I'm everything "adjacent" because words are hard to find these days.
  I'm living "life adjacent" right now.

APRIL 20, 2020

It's June 2012. I have just somehow been flown to New York to screen-test for *SNL* after doing a showcase in Chicago. It feels so crazy and unreal that I don't tell many people. I assume I won't get this job I don't even dare to dream about, so I try to take the audition as the win. I'm staying at a tiny hotel right by 30 Rock. I am terrified. I do my short audition at what I recognize as the stage where I've seen countless heroes hug each other at the *SNL* good nights. I always thought, *They must genuinely be so happy to live that life and end their week by hugging their friends before they all go to a fabulously fun party.* I'm on that stage after waiting in a small room by myself for what feels like eight hours. I have no idea what I'm doing.

I do three character pieces: a New York cruise ship passenger trying to bring a fresh pineapple back onto the ship with her and demanding to speak to someone in charge when they won't let her; a chubby little boy thanking his waitress at a diner after a Saturday family meal; and a Midwestern party aunt bragging about wearing her niece's size. Then I do three impressions: Elizabeth Dole handling hecklers; Rebecca Lobo, the WNBA star, trying her hand at standup, but it's really just her trying to sneeze because she has been told she sneezes funny; and a contestant from a 1997 episode of *ElimiDATE Milwaukee.*

ElimiDATE was one of those early dating shows before the big reality TV boom. I watched all of the reality TV before real reality TV, and I was crazy about it. There were the talk shows: Jenny Jones with her favorite sidekick, Rude Jude; Maury, who seemed to really enjoy bad teen girls, paternity disputes, and weird phobias (I have a funny memory of a woman who was afraid of olives, saying they reminded her of dead people); Sally Jessy Raphael, who would bring bad people onstage only so she could say "GET OFF MY STAGE" to thunderous applause; and of course Montel Williams, with his favorite medium Sylvia Browne, who, with the voice of a longtime chain smoker, would ask the audience, "Does someone here have a connection to the letter B? It is maybe a father figure."

I also watched all the early dating shows, which were always fascinating because no matter what the theme or rules of the show were, and no matter where the show was being filmed, they always ended up in a hot tub. I don't know where these places exist. I've never been to a club with a private hot tub room in the back. Did they film at a hotel? *ElimiDATE* was one of my favorites because they traveled to different cities throughout America and I enjoyed watching some of the worst people with different American regional accents. I remember one guy with a thick Wisconsin accent saying one of his favorite things to do was throw sticks in the street to hear the cars drive over them. He said it more than once.

During my audition, which I worry is too short now that I'm here on this stage, I think I hear some laughing. It's surprising and hopefully good news, as I was told they never laugh. Then I go back to a little room until they tell me it's time to go. It's late and I head back to the small hotel room, not sure what to do with myself. I feel like a zombie. What in the hell just happened? What am I supposed to be feeling? How am I supposed to feel normal in any way? I have forgotten my phone charger of course, so I can't call anyone after, trying to conserve the battery. I go to the airport early that morning and buy a cheap new charger.

When I get back to Chicago, my friend Susannah picks me up. She's driving us back home and I'm trying to tell her everything I can remember and I see I have an email from an *SNL* producer. They want me to fly back to New York to meet with "people" in the offices. Susannah and I freak out. My mom freaks out. My dad freaks out.

I fly back within the week. I go to 30 Rock and sit in the office of one of the producers, Lindsay

Shookus. I talk to her. John Mulaney comes in and I talk to him. I talk to Steve Higgins. I'm hoping I seem cool and collected and charming and funny and all the things I'm definitely not at this moment. I have explosive energy in me. After I'm sent back to the hotel, I'm ready to go out!

I contact my friend Graham, from Chicago, who now lives in New York. We took an improv class together and became fast friends. My good friend Mackenzie from college is also in New York. I ask both of them to come hang out.

And my little cousin Owen sends me a message. I haven't seen him in years! He's talking to me like we are old friends. He's around if I want to hang out. And I smile. Of course I want to hang out with Owen who I haven't seen in years! Why not? I'm on a roll!

Owen and Graham meet me at a Mexican restaurant and we have margaritas. I think Owen and Graham split dinner, treating me. Then we head to a private karaoke room Graham likes and we meet with Mackenzie. I keep checking in with Owen. Is he having fun? Does he like me? Does he like my friends? Does he want to go to the next place? He's grinning, walking along excitedly with us. We are all excited!

We get to karaoke. Graham and I sing some Fiona Apple. I do "Case of the Ex" by Mya. Then all of a sudden, I see Shaggy come up. Owen says, "Oh, this is me." Graham, Mackenzie, and I laugh hard at Owen being the quieter one, watching us, and finally deciding it's time to do his thing. And his thing happens to be Shaggy.

And he's got this fucking song *down*. Practiced! Rehearsed! He's so good!

We all cheer for him and he says he loves doing Shaggy at karaoke. I like my cousin. He's fun. My friends like him. We walk back to my hotel that night, Owen and Graham making sure I get there safe, and we all laugh as I'm screaming nonsense because I'm so happy.

Owen stuck around the whole night.

APRIL 22, 2020

I speak with a young girl from work named Remi. She's new. I have never really spoken with her. My friend Erin puts us in contact thinking maybe I can help.

Her mom is in the ICU in LA. She's terrified. She doesn't know what to do. She knows only what the doctors have said. She only knows her mom can't get the Ebola drug; she can't get the other drug until her TB test results come back, and everything is backed up. Remi can't be there with her. She doesn't know what COVID is or does. It was so fast. It feels like everyone is being forced to learn a new language in seventy-two hours. I talk to her. I tell her anything I can remember that calmed me down when Jack was so sick with this unpredictable and totally unknown illness and I was terrified. I am so sorry for this girl, for the hours she will spending wondering if she will lose her mom. And I want to be able to help.

I say, "Maybe I'm a better writer during a time when everyone is devastated. I'm a great voice of devastation. It wouldn't shock me." We laugh.

But then I think more. I haven't been able to write about Owen until now. I still don't quite know why, but I have some ideas. I didn't want to get it wrong. I didn't want to feel self-indulgent with my loss. I didn't want to claim it as *my* loss when so many others were hurting. Where would I share my writing? Instagram? And then there's this thought that I never wanted to share him if it wasn't in a way where I was also sharing love. Or I never wanted to make someone else sad. Because that is not how to share Owen. So maybe now that it seems everyone is scared and unsure and the world is upside down, I'm finally able to write about him. Because everyone is already going through something. So I'm just another voice.

APRIL 24, 2020

Last night, Kevin and Matt and I were eating another one of the dinners I'd made. I'm always on a damn diet and now it seems a little bit silly. I love pasta. I love cooking. I love red wine. We ordered six more bottles of this one we like from the local wine store that delivers. They are really good at social distancing, we comment.

APRIL 27, 2020

I don't know what week we are on anymore. Feels silly to keep track.

I just read a heartbreaking post by Alexis Morley. She lost her boyfriend, award-winning songwriter Adam Schlesinger, to COVID earlier this month. She explains waiting for his fever to break and making jokes through text when he went to the hospital. And then the unthinkable happened.

I text Jack: *I'm really really grateful you recovered.*

As I slip slowly into some kind of routine in this new normal, I am shaken by how much we say "when this is all over" because it hits me each time that the farther we get from the first week of March, the less I think this will all be over.

I just checked my phone to see if it was May yet.

And while I'm a part of that group of people who stay in a lot, and so some of this doesn't bother me as much as others, I am devastated when I think of what I miss. Walking to work. My wonderful doormen Les, Mervin, Mario, Javier, and John—and the dog treats they keep up front with them to give to Lucy and the other pups in my building after walks. My trips to Los

Angeles with Lucy on the plane with me. Dance parties. Going out to eat with friends.

We used to go to a Mexican restaurant all the time called Tacuba. They have great sautéed spicy kale. And spicy margaritas. We went for my birthday one year. They put flowers in my drink. My friend Mackenzie went to the bathroom as we were leaving and she had toilet paper on her shoe and I pointed it out as a fake "bullying" joke in the front of the restaurant but then we were all suddenly really laughing so hard, the staff too, with Mackenzie in the middle laughing so hard she was crying. Rashida wore heels that night, as she'd been starting to dress up more lately, and by the end of the night she could barely walk, but then my friend Shawn switched shoes with her. I have pictures and video of Shawn and Rashida walking next to each other wearing each other's shoes.

Jack and I met up one night at the Time Warner building to try to get a late dinner, although everything was closing early. I felt so embarrassed that I'd made him come uptown to a bunch of closed restaurants. They said they were open online! We finally got one place to serve us and we both were so overly thankful to the gruff waiter, who wasn't happy to be serving us. We joked afterward that it was so over-the-top of both of us that it was almost like we were trying to take him home.

I started going to an Italian restaurant near my apartment. I met up with Owen and Leda and Rashida for dinner there once. I was late, of course, and Owen was standing outside. "Hey, cuz." We hugged and then he gently said, "I think there was some kind of issue with the reservation maybe?" I checked my phone and realized I somehow totally fucked up everything I could have making a reservation: wrong date, wrong time, wrong number of people. "They said they are going to figure out how to get us in, though." And they did. And they gave us fried zucchini on the house.

I met Jack at a bar outside my work once. We were supposed to get a quick drink but we wound up staying there much longer because we were having fun and flirting and sitting next to each other on stools, so sort of touching legs every now and then between giggles about nothing, and every now and then I would dare to look him in the eyes, which is hard for me. And then he came to my work with me and let me do my favorite thing of showing my favorite videos of sketches on the server there. I liked that night.

I miss all the things I never thought I'd have to miss.

And I wonder if that's what's going to all be over soon.

But I do as I do every day, and I let the thought go.

APRIL 28, 2020

Everything in the world seems so chaotic and random right now, but because of this space, I keep feeling as if suddenly my own life is not as random but is full of all these connections and coincidences. I don't mean to say I believe in fate. I just mean I've always felt like the chaotic one trying to figure out how to fit into the world around me. Now in this isolation, it seems like the world is disjointed and figuring itself out, and I'm the one with some type of order, waiting on the world to find its axis again.

I made a video this week playing Michigan governor Gretchen Whitmer for the latest *SNL at Home*.

The governor (who I think is fabulous and smart and tough) responds that she liked the sketch (!!!), but I was drinking the wrong beer. I had her drinking a Labatt Blue instead of one of the many Michigan craft beers. I get an email saying she wants to send me a "Michigan treat." I think she's going to send some beer here. It's very cool.

I get defensive at first. I know Michigan has tons of craft beer! Of course! I remember friends driving across the border to get Bell's Oberon. That was how to be a beer snob in my Chicago suburb growing up: you knew your Michigan beer and would make the drive to get it.

I get a lot of nice messages today from people in Michigan on my Instagram. It makes me feel good. I want to say, "I love Michigan!" And I do love Michigan. I do feel a warmth, but I think it's just from lumping it in with my general connection to the Midwest. Or maybe the beautiful southeastern Michigan scenery from vacations with family and friends when I lived in Chicago.

And then I remember why I have this connection there. And what's behind the little tug on my heart when I think of Michigan.

Over the summer right after my freshman year of college in California I came back to Oak Park for my summer break. I was working as an intern for the company my dad worked for in Chicago. Trying to save some money. I saw a lot of friends that summer but missed one who was visiting because I bowed out of a party one Friday night. I was tired.

My friend Erica. She was living in Kalamazoo with her older brother John. She was a carefree goofball with a billion different hairstyles all throughout life. After the party I skipped, she went back to Kalamazoo. And one afternoon that July she went to get a sandwich from Jimmy John's. As she left the parking lot, her car was hit by a train.

I went to work the day I heard, in a daze. And then I think I was stuffing envelopes around a table and I said, "My friend was hit by a train and they don't know if she'll come out of her coma." The other interns stared at me.

"Maybe you should go home."

"Yeah, I think I should."

A large group of friends and family gathered at the hospital in Kalamazoo. I think I only went into her room once or twice. We held her hands and sang to her and forgot all the lyrics to every song. We slept on the floor in the lobby, and I would sometimes silently watch Erica's mom working away in her notebooks, drawing sketches of Erica's face.

We sat on the lawn outside of the hospital mostly. Just being with each other, trying to figure out how this was happening. It was sunny, and so it was the nicest spot to camp out while you waited for your friend to pass away. Every time I heard a helicopter, I'd make eye contact with another friend. We wondered if it was there for her organs. She was a donor. Always a generous person who took it upon herself to look out for the underdogs. There was a homeless man who was around her house a lot. She always gave him what she had if she could. I only know this because he gave her brother $5 after hearing what happened to her, to help if he could. He wanted to give back to her.

A radio station in Kalamazoo gave us a shout-out one day. They dedicated "Always Something There to Remind Me" to all "the people on the lawn." We got tattooed at a local shop in Kalamazoo. All of us got the same symbol for laughter along with her initials, "EER," but we got the tattoo on different parts of our bodies. I chose the back of my neck. It felt like a loving spot—a spot where I often remembered my dad mindlessly massaging me as we sat next to each other watching TV growing up.

I went to the Jimmy John's and found pieces of her headlight and held them and stared at them in my little hand, wondering if I should keep them or not. A man and woman stopped their car and came out to us, my friends and me, crying in the road. They saw the little pink memorial on a light post. She loved pink. The woman looked at me. "Was that your friend?" I nodded. "I'm so so sorry." And she hugged me for a long time.

Years later, I went door-to-door for Barack Obama in Kalamazoo with my dad and my step-mom and one of the nameless faceless boys I dated in Chicago. I wanted to visit the Jimmy John's.

You see, that particular crossing had seen over 140 or so accidents because it was on a weird angle and it was hard to see any oncoming traffic because of the trees. And the signal wasn't working. Jimmy John's was the only thing on that side of the tracks.

After Erica's accident, though, they fixed it. And I remember crying that day I went back and saw the improvements. You saved people, Erica.

Her birthday is April 4, two days before Owen's. It's been seventeen years since she left us. And Saturday, I finally got to give a shout-out back to Michigan.

Thank you, Michigan. I'll get the beer right next time.

MAY 3, 2020

It's raining and gloomy today. I text Jack: *Why doesn't whoever's in charge of everything know the weather is a big determining factor in how my days feel?!*

It's jarring watching TV right now. Everything that looks clear and doesn't sound tinny makes me think of "before." And again, I wonder how long my only way of connecting with people will be through so many screens and wires. I've never loved connecting that way. I was allowed to be stubborn about it before. Now I have no other option.

Matt has been doing these theater classes over Zoom. He was explaining an exercise he did the other day and said they paired off and looked each other in the eyes and played the mirror game. I feel like screaming, "YOU AREN'T LOOKING ANYONE IN THE EYES! YOU ARE LOOKING AT A SCREEN! AND THERE'S A LAG IN ZOOM SO YOU AREN'T MIRRORING ANYONE."

That lag makes me think today that we are not living in the same time as each other. Communicating that way means we are always communicating from the future. There's not a "real time" option. It makes me miss everyone even more. I feel so alone.

I've never really been good at looking people in the eyes. It's a challenge. I have social anxiety and I do this thing involuntarily where when I'm talking to someone, they think I'm looking at their forehead. It makes for a lot of awkward interactions. I have made a lot of men suddenly self-conscious about their hairlines. And then I get immediately self-conscious explaining, "No, I'm not looking at your forehead. I have social anxiety and I'm not always able to look people in the eyes and I never know when it's happening." I immediately create a vulnerable and intimate situation and I don't want that with most new people I'm meeting.

A couple years ago I took a vacation to Seville and Ibiza with my friend Mackenzie. She was my travel companion for a while. She's a great companion for me. She's naturally very social, and I like having people like that around me because I've always felt incapable of being good at talking to strangers.

In Seville, we find this "secret" after-hours spot Bicicleteria. Her English friend with a funny lisp tells us about it. He says we need a password ("pathword") to get in. Turns out being young and female is even better than a password. Mackenzie easily talked us in. We go twice.

The first night we sit with a group of travelers from a nearby hostel in this dimly lit, smoky room. It's sort of red, the lighting. The bar serves what they have until they run out. People are passing around a joint. There's a boy who sticks out to me because I don't like his energy. He's smug and kind of rude to everybody. In my head, I turn him into a rich prep school asshole. I have no idea if he is rich or in school. At one point he turns to Mackenzie and says, "Your face is weird." What a nasty little brat. I don't like him. Later, he turns to me and says something like, "What do you know? You're so drunk you can't even look me in the eyes." I'm not so drunk. And he doesn't get to know about my anxiety.

I stare at him with a frightened look on my face and say, "No. I can't look you in the eyes because there's nothing there. It's just black, you know? I can't see anything there." He laughs uncomfortably. I stay staring. "I'm not joking. It's terrifying." He doesn't know how to respond. *I can look you in the eyes now,* I think. He ends up leaving not long after. I am so proud of myself.

The next night we go back and we are sitting alone. It's a bit early, so people are still sort of flowing in. A handsome boy walks past. We make eye contact—quickly, of course—across the room a couple of times. I hope he'll come over. And he does. He introduces himself. He's Italian. Marco. He's dressed like a professor: black sweater over a button-up shirt, dress pants, nice shoes that look dressy but lived in. He travels alone. He's studying to be a diplomat. What the hell does that mean? He laughs when I buy him a drink as a peace offering because of our two countries' disagreement over Amanda Knox.

He kisses me that night on the roof of our Airbnb. There's a tiny *piscina* up there we never end up using. He's so Italian and he keeps dramatically saying, "You're so soft. Your skin is so soft, oh my God." I laugh but I'm secretly totally swooning.

He is on his way to another city in two days. And we are going to Ibiza. Marco and I exchange WhatsApp numbers. I talk to him a lot. For hours a day. I wind up breaking my foot my first night in Ibiza, when I'm trying to "take it easy" and have a more relaxed, early night. I miss a step after getting bottles of Coke from a bar because I don't want to drink alcohol that night. Mackenzie took half an ecstasy and she keeps asking to borrow people's jackets because she's so cold. I don't think it's a good idea for two girls on their own to be messed up in Ibiza. I have been immediately on alert since we've gotten here. I look at everyone who approaches us and try to determine whether or not they're a sex trafficker.

Anyway, I miss a small step and my damn foot breaks. I have always had this vasovagal response thing where I faint when I see my own blood but also sort of whenever I feel any kind of trauma. I start to faint at the table. We are with two Irish girls named Laura and now they are stuck with a fainting person who can't walk on her own and this person on ecstasy who is close to tears about being cold.

I sob all night when I get back to the hotel. I can't believe I broke my fucking foot on my first night here. Not only that, I'm going immediately back to *SNL* when I'm home. How will I do it with a broken foot?

Marco texts me in the morning, *Buongiorno principessa*, like Roberto Benigni in *Life Is Beautiful*. Marco constantly reminds me of Roberto Benigni. He talks passionately and he's over-the-top with a gleam in his eye as if he knows he's putting it on a little. I like it.

I go to a clinic the next morning. They want to give me a hard cast, but I keep saying, "No. Soy actriz," because it turns out most of the Spanish I learned from a couple months of practicing on Duolingo before the trip involved eating apples and not breaking one's foot. They don't give me a hard cast but make me promise to go immediately to a foot doctor when I'm back in New York in less than a week (where I'll end up getting a walking boot).

I spend most of the rest of the trip indoors with my foot wrapped in bandages and on crutches. So I spend a lot of the time getting to know this funny Italian. We talk about music and family and movies and language and travel, and by the time

I get home, we are sending each other childhood pictures. We talk every day. Always ending before five p.m. my time because he's always asleep by eleven or so his time. Sometimes that frustrates me. I get lonely at night in my time zone and I wish I could talk to him then.

I go to Rome for a week that fall with friends to visit him. He makes a trip to New York for New Year's Eve. The first couple of days are nice and then I start feeling annoyed with him in my little apartment. It feels like we lost the connection and can't get it back, and I start to resent him for taking up so much of my little space. I feel guilty, but I don't even want him to kiss me. We have two talks where I "break up" whatever we had. He is as dramatic about this as everything else. I don't mean *dramatic* in a mean way. He's just always a little more than most people I know. He says he's heartbroken. I feel awful.

Two months later he sends me an Italian book. There's a Polaroid inside. It's me, but just my back really, and just a sliver of the side of my face. He caught me right as I was turning away. I'm turning away from him in the photo. This is how he sees me.

I wonder if I'll ever be able to be with another person or if it's just not for me.

On April 1 this year, I send Marco a message on Instagram. I haven't seen him or spoken to him in about five years.

"I don't know where you are or how you are or if it's shallow to send a message now, but I know I went through a rough time and my life has changed very much in three weeks. So I'm thinking of you and hope you and your family are all safe. And I know how much traveling means to you, so I imagine this is even more difficult. Sending my thoughts and love and solidarity from across the way in New York."

I wonder how he will feel about me reaching out. He responds that night: "Hi Cec, it's not shallow at all."

He goes on and says he's in Rome and he's safe and then he goes into a lengthy discussion about the government response in Italy and how the way of life has changed, and he's written so much, always too much, which makes me laugh. The second giant paragraph starts with "According to the media . . ." That's Marco.

At the end of the note, though, I tear up a little. He says: "I know how sensitive you are and I hope you're not suffering too much. I send all my love and thoughts."

I'm still soft to him.

And that does, in fact, soften me. I tell him about Owen and my anxiety and the house in the woods. He says: "I can't imagine how hard it has been to fight fear and pain alone." We talk about Cuomo. Marco tells me not to worry too much: "It's going to be a beautiful summer."

We leave the conversation there, with another lengthy message about philosophy from Marco. I decide that's a good way to end it.

We haven't talked since. But I'm glad I had the connection. Five years ago and four weeks ago.

I feel slightly less alone.

MAY 11, 2020

I haven't written in a week. Been doing a lot of work for *SNL*. And I'm still so tired. The days are unpredictable and bizarre even though they seem so insignificant nobody can tell you what day it is. What a combo. May 6, for instance: I woke up and I checked my phone to discover my landlord Howard had passed away from COVID in April. His daughter emailed me. I said how sorry I was. She mentioned how fond he was of me. And I liked him too. He made me laugh, because Howard had clearly typed my very long lease on a typewriter as opposed to a computer and preferred real mail over email. (I have never liked the term *snail mail* but I especially don't like it now, because it feels dismissive of anything that doesn't involve modern technology and I really miss things that don't involve modern technology. Plus it seems most of the world is moving slower these days anyway, so the expression seems weirdly outdated.)

Then two hours later I was filming something for *SNL*. After that, a good friend since second grade texted me: *My dad just got taken to the ER with a fever. We can't be with him.* My heart sank. I texted my parents. *Fuck. He can't have covid.* I tried to be optimistic about this virus that's taken so many so quickly. I filmed another bit for *SNL at Home*. Right before bed, my friend texted me that her dad tested negative for COVID. He had a kidney infection. I was so relieved! I laughed with Matt and Kevin about how strange it is to be so relieved to hear someone has a kidney infection. What a day.

MAY 12, 2020

I get a text from Megan informing me that some-one made a reservation for the Airbnb for June. She's sorry she can't keep it for us, but this is a long-term rental. She's been letting us sort of "play it by ear" up until now. We'd extend for a couple weeks or a couple of months. I don't know when I'll be back in the city. I know I'm not ready.

I knew this day would come, but I was hoping to put it off a little longer, I suppose. I sit with Kevin and Matt and bring up maybe staying in the Hudson Valley. I need to hear what the words sound like I guess. I need to say it out loud. I'm not going back.

I find a new rental house on Airbnb. It's in Rhinebeck. I had lunch there once with my friend Kent who writes for *SNL*. It seemed nice. I reserve it for June and part of July.

I thank Megan for everything. She's sorry to see us go. She offers to sell me the house as her Realtor friend convinced her to put it on the market. It's a good time to sell if you have a house in the woods. I can't buy a house now. It's a nice thought for a second. But it's not real. Although I don't know what's real right now, to be honest. I can't think about a home. I'm scared of my home.

Later, she texts that she's going to bring me potting soil and some planter pots. She says she has extra.

In case I need them for my new "little garden."

She's talking about the little basil plants I have just placed outside on the deck near my bedroom.

I don't really know what I'm doing.

But Megan wants to help of course. She likes to encourage me to do things outside, in the sun. She's offered me bikes, kayaks, board games, hikes, dinners and lunches from her restaurant. A home.

And now, even though she can't offer me her home anymore, she's on her way with soil.

She's still helping me plant my roots.

MAY 13, 2020

My dad sends me an email today. Owen's website is going up this Friday. People can post pictures and writings and his music. There will be a section of just his day-to-day "things," like maybe a picture of Owen's favorite shirt. I love all of this, but I know I'm not ready to just click on it yet. I'll take my time. I know I've only dipped my toes into the grief over Owen's loss. I'm not ready to dive in fully. I'm worried there's a good chance I'll drown.

A stink bug flew at my head and landed inside the lampshade today. I *flew* off the bed. I am so afraid of bugs. All of them. But I also don't like to kill anything. I sobbed for hours after spraying a wasp nest once. I joke all the time that I'm a Zen Buddhist. I caught the stink bug in a glass and held thick paper over the top so I could very slowly and carefully walk it outside. I'm trying to be quiet because Megan and her partner are planting new flowers in the pots out front on the deck. I set the stink bug glass out back and the glass of course immediately shatters. The bug is okay, the glass is not. Oh well. I'm not a perfect Zen Buddhist.

I had a Zen Buddhist friend once. Her name was Megu. I met her my senior year in high school.

At my art school. My last of three high schools.

I went to public school and enjoyed most of my classes and did lots of theater. I bought my first bag of pot with my best friend Liz my sophomore year. It was just as you'd imagine the first bag of pot a fifteen-year-old would buy in 1999. It was full of stems and seeds and I really didn't know what to do with it, seeing as buying rolling papers and rolling a joint was laughably out of my league. I didn't have anything to smoke out of either, as I wasn't yet brave enough to go to a "head shop" in the city. You had to be eighteen in there, right? And honestly I didn't know any weed lingo, and that was almost scarier. Having to say "bowl" or "pipe" or "one-hitter," and did I say "weed" even? Did people say "pot"? Would people think I was a loser if I said the wrong word? I mean, it's sort of astonishing I ever bought pot in the first place because of my fear over not following the rules and getting into trouble. I was one of the only people among my friends and acquaintances who never even had a fake ID. I used one exactly once in my life, borrowed from a friend's older sister. I was twenty. I was months away from being of legal drinking age, but here I was with a racing pulse, full of anxiety that I was doing something illegal. The whole time I was pretending to be having fun with some friends at one of the local bars on the "strip" in the town next to mine. Oak Park was dry, so all of the bars were in a town called Forest Park. I went to the "strip" off and on as an adult, home from school, but mainly just to see if I somehow would finally feel like I "fit in" with everyone I had thought was so cool in high school. I never did.

But anyway, I had this bag of pot that would never be rolled or packed or smoked or anything by me, and it felt pretty rebellious and grown-up just to have it in my possession. It's probably why I agreed to keep it in my book bag. I put it in there right after we bought it, and a day later I went to callbacks for *The Shadow Box* after school. I really wanted to be Beverly.

The morning after the audition, I was called to security. They had found my book bag outside of the school sitting near a door. I had asked another friend (not Liz) to put my back pack in the greenroom. I guess my friend never got it to the greenroom for me. I hadn't even noticed, let alone worried. Too excited about the auditions. I never quite understood how my backpack ended up outside the door, and it was never something that really mattered because it felt like that would be looking to blame someone else and it didn't change what happened.

Security opened the book bag up when they found it, to see who it belonged to, and found the little bag of crappy pot. They already knew what was in it when I got to the office. But for some reason, they pretended they hadn't gone through the bag. I'll never understand this and it always makes me uncomfortable. It was like they were playing a game with me. They opened every pocket except for the one holding the little seedy first bag of weed I'd ever bought. They even said, "I guess you can go." And as I got up, they said, "Oh, wait a minute. We forgot one pocket." It felt like a nightmare.

While I was being expelled, before being walked through the halls in handcuffs with a police officer, I asked if they could check the cast list for *The Shadow Box*. One of the security guards did me that bit of kindness and told me I had in fact been cast as Beverly. Sometimes I look back and wonder whether it was good to know or whether it made things more hurtful. I think I like having a small victory during what was such a difficult and humiliating day.

The rest of the day, and truthfully a lot of life at that time, is a bit hazy in my memory. I think it's because I sort of shut down at the time, and so I was hardly present. So it's difficult to try to remember what it was like to be there twenty years later when, at the time, I was trying so hard to *not* be there. I know I was taken to a police station and spent time in a little room (cell?) before my parents arrived. I will always appreciate the way my parents treated the whole thing. They had of course smoked pot in their lifetime and maybe were still partaking around this time. They also knew that school was important to me and I worked hard. So seeing me at the police station that afternoon, still crying, they felt sorry for me instead of angry with me. Of course they weren't totally okay with smoking weed as a teenager, and I was definitely grounded for a while, but they didn't punish me much beyond that. I think they also knew I was being punished plenty by the school.

I got out of going to court by agreeing to a program set up for kids in my situation. I realize I am much luckier here than a lot of kids because I grew up white and middle-class. Because I was a minor and the amount of weed was so small, my arrest would be expunged if I agreed to one hundred hours of community service. I spent a big chunk of my summer working at a wonderful community center for HIV-positive residents in my town. They helped to provide assistance with housing, finances, transportation—basically all of the nonmedical concerns of their clients.

I had to take a workshop before I started, and I remember a particularly emotional exercise we did where each of us in the class was given five index cards and told to write down the five most important things in our life: family, education, religion, career, etc. Then we placed the cards facedown and our neighbor removed two of the cards. We were told to pick up the three cards we had remaining. And then the instructor said something like, "You were diagnosed with HIV three months ago. This is what you still have and what you have lost because of your diagnosis." Then we discussed how we thought we could have lost these important parts of our life. A lot of the workshop was like this. I had certain ideas about the gravity and danger of the medical/physical ramifications of being HIV positive but had not really ever thought about the gravity and danger of the social stigma of being HIV positive.

My job consisted of working in reception and helping to stock the food pantry that was used as a sort of grocery store for the clients. I was also in charge of organizing the various contraception delivered to the center. I remember making piles of flavored condoms, dental dams, magnum condoms, ribbed, you name it. There was always a basket in the front of the office full of condoms for people to freely take. Some local kids found out, of course, and I remember one afternoon a group of about five eleven-to-twelve-year-old boys walking in and giggling while they hovered at the door for a second, before the "bravest" one grabbed a handful and declared, "I'm gonna get some pussy tonight." I remember my boss, when I mentioned this to her, just sighed and said, "Those have probably all been blown up into balloons by now." She was cool.

While expelled, I opted out of going to the

behavioral disorder school in Chicago that my school so graciously recommended. Instead, I went to Catholic school for a semester. I wasn't raised Catholic so it was a totally new world for me in a lot of ways. Especially a Catholic school right outside of Chicago. The majority of my classmates seemed to be Italian or Irish girls. I was fascinated by these beautiful long melodic Italian names (I had no idea what a confirmation name was before this) and all of the indoor tanning stories (poor Jo went twice one weekend because she couldn't say no to her boyfriend Kenny's mom wanting to take her, and so she burned her butt so badly it hurt sitting that Monday morning we were back in class in our scratchy skirts) and the planner notebooks covered in pictures of boys posing with tough-guy faces and big muscles from the brother school St. Patrick's (St. P's).

That semester, I got a letter telling me I was a National Merit Commended Scholar based on the PSAT test I had taken earlier that year at my public school. I would not be able to attend the ceremony at the public school though, as I was not allowed within a three-block radius or, I was told, the police would be called.

My junior year I was allowed to come back to the public school. But I wasn't okay. I didn't feel good. I started to feel really bad. I stopped going to classes that weren't the four I really cared about or rehearsals for a new play I was doing after school. (I can't remember the name. Tough time for my memory.) I shared a car with my brother, and so many nights I thought about doing one of two things: I would get on the freeway and drive west until I got to somewhere warm and welcoming, or I would drive home to sit in the garage with the car running, leaving the heat on so I was warm and comfy, and listen to my favorite mix tapes before I went to sleep and didn't have to wake up.

My mom sent me to our family psychiatrist. I liked her. She told me I was looking at the world through "shit-colored glasses." But still, school was more and more uncomfortable. I had never felt like I knew how to be one of these kids who seemed so normal, and now there was an even bigger gulf between us. I didn't know how to voice any of the panicked screaming in my head. I was only happy doing theater there.

A week before tech started for another show I was doing that spring, the head of the theater program asked me to drop out of the show. The school administration was unhappy about how I'd cut my class schedule down so much and thought I shouldn't be allowed to be in a school production. I was called into a meeting with my mother, and as we sat in the theater head's office, he smiled sympathetically at me and said that although I wouldn't be doing the show, they'd put a flyer in the program about "teen depression." I assumed that was also the reason they'd give to my castmates as to why I dropped out right before we opened—why, with only a week to recast my part, they'd now have to put in so much extra work after so many rehearsals. As if that would make it all okay and not totally destroy that last connection I had left at my high school. I remember feeling this bizarre split in that moment—intense panic deep down that made me want to scream, "ARE YOU FUCKING KIDDING ME?!?!" but also like my body was frozen and shut down, unable to feel much or even speak. My mom, sensing this, I suppose, put her hand on my arm and leaned over to whisper to me, "Please don't run out of this room."

Not long after that, I dropped out completely. Though I had been an A student my whole life, because of what I'd missed I was going to have to be a fifth-year senior, in order to get enough gym credits and credit for a class called Consumer Education that would satisfy the school's graduation requirements.

I spent afternoons in a local park near the library. A group of small kids would come by often for their recess. I loved seeing the games they made up. It usually involved two teams finding weapons to use against each other and then battling until most got bored and split off in little groups, except for the one kid who was not good at reading the room and continued to run screaming at everyone.

Some days I'd go inside the library and open any book I found interesting. Old science manuals. Short stories by D. H. Lawrence and Edith Wharton. A collection of essays about humans and the way they interact with animals. Psychology and sociology books. Virginia Woolf essays. Just chapters at a time. Pieces of things I found interesting that day. The homeschooling of the depressed kid who fell through the cracks.

I wasn't sure how or if I'd ever graduate. But my dad found an art school in Chicago. I auditioned that summer for my senior year. I got in. I was ecstatic. I'd been saving up money for college by working at a local coffee shop and doing various acting jobs: a McDonald's commercial that never aired, a driver's ed video for the state of Wisconsin, a video for kids about how to deal with alcoholic parents, an antismoking PSA. I used those savings to help pay tuition for my senior year at the Chicago Academy for the Arts. It was absolutely worth it to me.

I immediately loved the art school and the students. They felt like "my people." Weird and wonderful and all so talented. I loved (most of) the teachers. I felt like I couldn't fall through bureaucratic cracks there. I did correspondence courses so I could graduate on time. I smiled again. I went from not being able to speak for months to getting voted best personality at the end of the year.

But most important, I made good friends. I became particularly close with one person.

Megu.

I, along with a group of several others, was asked to look out for the new Japanese foreign exchange student. She was staying in a home in Oak Park. So I started talking to her.

Megu was half Japanese and half Bangladeshi. She was tiny and wore little flannel shirts and cardigans and came up to my armpit and had short hair, which she permed. She said it was to look like Bob Dylan. She had one front tooth that stuck out, and I never knew if she was being silly on purpose when she'd say, "I have to brush my tooth." Her English wasn't great but she didn't seem to care. She seemed to find me funny enough, too, and we hung out more and more. We used her electronic translator, which I called Kancho after learning that it sort of meant "butt sex" in Japanese slang. She pretended to roll her eyes at that, but then about a month later she was saying things like, "Oh no, I left Kancho at home."

As we became closer friends, I invited her to move into our little guest room. She was paying more than her family could necessarily afford to live in one room in this other house. So she started living with my mom and me and my big dog Emma. My mom had sort of an open-door policy of sharing her home with friends who might need a place for a while. I'd like to think this is something she's passed on to me as well. And we had extra room as my brother was away at college for most of the year and my dad had moved out years before. My mom was very open about her plans to eventually sell the house and move into a smaller condo, but she was hoping to hold out until my brother and I were firmly settled elsewhere.

Megu's room was next to mine, and most nights I'd hear her humming (I distinctly remember a lot of "I've Got the World on a String") as she'd paint self-portraits or make little bug figures out of things she'd found outside. She found long branches and soaked them so they'd bend. Then she painted them black and stretched them over her bed like a canopy.

We got better at talking to each other through Kancho, and I found out about Megu's school history. She hadn't had a normal high school career either. See, most of her schooling was in the hospital. Megu had had cancer. She showed me her passport photo one day, which she hadn't shown anyone else. She still had that funny tooth sticking out, but she had no hair. Her short Bob Dylan perm took on a new meaning.

She stayed in my house for two years, even

when I went to college. Just Megu and my mom and dog. My mom would call me and say, in a loving way, "Megu is so weird," and Megu would call and say to me, in a loving way, "Your mom is so weird." They were both absolutely right.

One summer after she'd returned from a visit to Japan, Megu pulled me aside at my boyfriend Henry's beautiful beach home in Michigan. She said, "I have to tell you something." With light help from Kancho, I learned Megu's mom had gone to a "witch doctor." I only say that because we don't quite have the words. Maybe more of a shaman. Her mother walked in and without her saying much, this man said, "Your daughter doesn't have cancer." He gave her a small sachet for Megu to wear around her neck for protection. Megu showed me. She was smiling, sort of glowing. Megu felt free. She felt "well" finally. I told her that was amazing. She smiled at me for a beat and said, "Yeah . . . So I can smoke pot now."

Megu moved back to Tokyo permanently the summer after my freshman year of college. I never got a proper goodbye, though. The week before Megu left, Erica's car was hit by the train in Kalamazoo, so I drove out to sit with friends on the hospital lawn.

Megu went home. I went back to school in California. Somehow her address got lost in the house while I was away. We couldn't find any new contact information for her. There was no social media really (not that Megu would ever take part!). Every other year or so for about ten years, I did a search for her online, which was very difficult without Kancho.

But then, Megu was a Zen Buddhist. I think I learned enough from her to know this story isn't a sad story. We were lucky to meet when we did, and how nice to have this special friendship and funny stories to tell about this wonderful bizarre little person. I got to see Megu feel freedom from sickness finally one day, and she got to see me start smiling and laughing again.

We didn't lose each other. We found each other.

Owen would've liked Megu.

MAY 17, 2020

I've started planting basil.

I've never planted anything before, although I have a fake tree that I love, left in my apartment by my wonderful landlord Howard. This is so new to me, in fact, that I forgot to also buy soil and pots. I had this tray of basil sitting outside and then inside for a week. Inside, because I read basil needs to be warm. But now I've got three pots (a fourth on its way courtesy of Amazon) and two mugs, and I'm willing this basil to grow, to not die under my care. I ask Kevin every day if he thinks it looks good. He assures me it does. "Look at those happy leaves!"

When I was growing up, both of my parents were excellent gardeners. I never quite inherited their green thumbs. They loved going to our local nursery, Frank's, and buying new plants and flowers every year. Our yard was small but always full of flowers and bushes and vegetables. We had peonies that blossomed by April or May. I know this because this was always my end-of-year gift for my teachers.

Next to the peonies was a butterfly bush. That plant attracted lots of butterflies but also lots of bees. I got mad about something or other as a kid and went outside and wrapped my fingers around a bee to get stung. That would show my mom.

We had a raspberry bush, and we could pick fresh raspberries right off the stem and eat them. I think I liked the novelty of getting to eat raspberries right off the bush more than I liked raspberries themselves. My dad had a giant bleeding heart bush that sat loudly and proudly in the corner like royalty. We had bright orange poppies. Snapdragons. Lilies of the valley. Crocuses. Rhododendrons. Lilacs and honeysuckle. Forget-me-nots. My parents at one point put a trellis on our porch, and we had morning glory growing up the front of the house. We had tulips running along the side of the house. My mom had an herb garden, and the mint was another one I got to eat right from the ground. Rosemary. ("Run it through your fingers, Cecily. Doesn't that smell good?") Thyme. Basil. Tomatoes wrapped around wooden sticks! I think cucumbers, too.

Just remembering them all now I'm blown away by how committed my parents were. I can't believe I remember all these names. I can't believe I remember where each of the flowers was planted in my yard. I knew where all the roses were planted because that's where I found my mom the day in fifth grade when I ran home from school because I told a boy I'd "go with him" and he put his arm around me and I pretended to like it but

135

inside I felt terrible. I wasn't ready to "go with" someone. Why were all my classmates ready to date and kiss, even *French* kiss, and I wasn't?

My favorite part of our garden, though, was a purple plum tree in the front yard. It was the perfect size for an eight-year-old who couldn't climb trees. I would sit in a little nook between two thick purple branches and wonder if I'd ever get to eat the plums before the squirrels. We had big fir bushes lining the front of the house, like a gentleman's beard. One time my magenta "Pizzazz" bicycle was stolen from our garage. Months later I discovered it had been returned, thrown into those bushes with a giant hole in the tire.

Speaking of bicycles: I have always had a blurry memory that I saw a kid I didn't recognize from school have some kind of awful bike accident on the playground. I remember it as his handle impaling him. I was haunted by this image of a big hole in a kid's stomach. But that can't be right, right? Memories are funny.

Back to my garden.

One day my brother, Nat, and my dad had a really bad fight. This was not out of the ordinary in my house. My brother had ADHD, ADD, depression, dyslexia, learning disabilities, Asperger's. He was very overweight. All those "disorders" that just get you labeled as a bad kid. Especially in the nineties. My dad and Nat would have loud screaming matches, and my mom would hold me in her room because they scared me. After this particularly bad fight, my brother went missing. For hours. We searched the streets around the house, yelling for him, and called neighbors. We almost called the police. He came back around dusk, just walked through the door. Turns out he was sitting under the porch all along, hiding behind the morning glory.

My brother and I would fight, too. Physically sometimes. I bit him hard once in the armpit. That was the only time I ever got a hit in. He was bigger and stronger, so most of our fights he was chasing me around the table, where I could fend him off for a while. I wasn't ever really scared, though. I loved my brother dearly. I knew he loved me. One night he had taken a little axe from wherever we kept an axe for some reason and was going at the lock my parents had started using on the fridge doors to keep Nat from overeating. I sat at the kitchen table right next to him, silently watching him. My mom yelled for me to come upstairs. But I didn't this time. My brother turned to me and said, "I wouldn't ever hurt you." And I said, "I know." My brother was the sweetest and funniest person I knew—still is. He's a really good guy with a big heart that he didn't get to share with many people for a long time.

As you can imagine, school was not a very

kind place for my brother. I don't quite know the extent to which he was bullied, but I remember hearing some on the playground. For being fat, for not being able to read as well as other kids. Kids would make jokes to me as if I'd find them funny. He was put in some special classes, which must have been very frustrating for a guy who is so intelligent and now works in IT.

He started seeing a psychiatrist at one point. Sometimes I'd go along for family sessions. I remember the building had huge ornate metal doors and a black-and-white checkered floor. Later on, I would start seeing this same psychiatrist. She prescribed him Ritalin for his ADD. The pills worked until the day he yelled upstairs, "Mom, I think I have to go to the hospital. I swallowed my whole bottle of pills." We spent hours in the Oak Park Hospital that night. They made my brother throw up to get rid of the pills in his stomach. I saw him sitting up on his hospital bed in the ER, exhausted and crying. I spent the night at the house of my mom's best friend. Later we found a note he'd written. I only remember that he wanted to leave all of his money to Planned Parenthood.

He was admitted to the children's psych ward at Rush hospital in Chicago for a week. I can't quite remember what it looked like there. I can vaguely remember seeing children's drawings taped onto the white walls. It smelled like disinfectant.

He had art classes and daily therapy. We had a couple family sessions. Being the youngest, and seemingly "okay," I wasn't always involved in those sessions.

After the week, my brother came home. He went back to school. My parents spent a few weeks still seeing his counselor, but on their own. And after one of those sessions, I sat on the couch by the back door, waiting and watching for them from the window as I normally did when they were out. I saw my mom walk out of the garage first, quickly with her head down. My dad followed slowly behind her, his head down as well. They asked to talk to my brother and me, and so we all gathered in my room, Nat and I on my bed, them standing in front of us on my pink carpet. And then my parents said they were getting separated. My dad would be moving out.

In the years after my dad left, the garden began to slowly fall apart. My mom still did her best to keep up with her favorite flowers, but it was hard to find the time as she was back in school to become a nurse and then eventually a nurse practitioner. She did this while raising two kids full-time except for "Thursday night and every other weekend." I remember the yard becoming messier, disheveled. These long vines dangled over the little cement walkway near the roses where I told her about going with a boy. I hated these vines and branches because they were always just in the way, tangling me and catching my arms like someone trying to keep me from leaving an upsetting conversation. Some sections were empty, or sparse at best. I tried to plant wildflowers near the roses once but I didn't do much more than scatter the bag of seeds. So they never really became the lavish garden pictured on the front of the seed packet. My plum tree got a disease and the city cut it down. My mom replaced it with a little apple tree, but it wasn't purple and there was no longer a nook for me. My dad's bleeding hearts were gone.

My mom sold the house eventually, downsizing to a two-bedroom apartment. She made sure to find a place with a little balcony facing south. She has all of her plants out there. It's harder to maintain, though, as she spends half her time living in a condo in Puerto Vallarta. She saved up for a long time to get that condo in Mexico, and she's enjoying her retirement there as much as she can—although she never seems to stop working in some way: volunteering at local schools teaching English or helping with food drives and whatever else may come her way. I had to beg her not to return to work as a nurse at the start of COVID, because I was scared with her age and a heart condition she's developed. She and I share a love of the sun and the beach. She's down there now, during this quarantine, unhappy that they closed the pools and beaches. I try to tell her it won't be forever and she should sit on her balcony, where she can still enjoy the sun she loves so much. My brother watches her apartment when she's gone. Along with his girlfriend. He's madly in love, finally getting to really share his big heart with someone.

My dad lives in a house across town and he is still an avid gardener. He likes big statement pieces like clay fireplaces and stone Buddhas. (And, yes, it's totally that older-white-guy self-help cliché thing, but I figure I've teased him enough about it over the years and so now I can just appreciate the statues for actually being really lovely.) He can spend hours sitting out in his yard. He even got remarried in that backyard. My two friends followed me down the alley as I cried that day after the ceremony. Not because I didn't appreciate and love my new family: my stepmom, Colleen, who loved me so much and told me often, and my two stepsiblings, Steve and Sammi, both of whom I adored. It was just an official ending to the life and family I once had. And I was sad for my mom.

Now here I am today in this room in my rental house in the Hudson Valley with three pots and two mugs of basil sitting next to the south-facing window. I'm hoping I can take care of something else. I am doing okay with Lucy, I think, and trying to always get better at taking care of myself. I haven't always been very good at it. So we'll see.

And suddenly I remember the daffodils.

Laurel planted daffodils the day Owen was born.

I hope someday I can plant daffodils at a place that I call my home.

MAY 20, 2020

The last *SNL at Home* airs tonight.

It's been really hard to make this show. We've set up a mini studio and it seems I'm working all day. I'm doing my hair and makeup and trying to make costumes out of whatever was in my suitcase and whatever the wardrobe department finds on Amazon that can be shipped quickly. Kevin makes all my props. He's a good little artist!

We film the final scene all together in the guest room upstairs. Matt holds my phone to film. He's wearing an earpiece so he can hear our director Paul, who is watching through some new technology I had to download that lets *SNL* into my phone so they can see what I'm filming in real time. It seems crazy to let your phone be hacked, but I'm not worried about normal worrisome things right now. It's too exhausting.

We are filming a scene in bed. Kevin has reheated a slice of pizza we used earlier as a prop. It's supposed to be like a real New York slice of pizza: big and greasy and cheesy and delicious. We are making a scene about being in the city again. Dreaming we are doing all of the things we miss in New York. I'm seeing a Broadway show. And eating a slice of pizza. I didn't write the sketch, my friends Kent and Anna did, but they sure got me right.

The sketch is especially poignant because just as we cannot be in the city doing any of these things, we can't make a sketch or video or our show like we normally do. So my quarantine roommate films me on my iPhone as *SNL*'s director watches from his computer somewhere wherever he is, and I'm holding a small, hard, burnt piece of pizza made in our oven. In a guest bedroom at an Airbnb in the Hudson Valley.

Lucy is in the shot. She's not an actress. She always seems to know when I'm trying to take a picture of her and turns her head away, immediately stopping whatever funny thing she was doing that made me want to get a photo or video. She's no different now. My director, watching through my phone, asks if I can get her to bark or make a sound. She's normally pretty talkative but of course will not make any sound right now and doesn't seem to even want to be on this bed anymore. We get what we can. *SNL at Home* is a "get what we can" show right now.

I watch the sketch that night. It's really amazing. They've put the whole cast back in the city, through our at-home green screens. I watch as my castmates seem to be waving goodbye to me. Before I wake up again in my bed, with my dog, realizing it was just a dream. But I'm still holding this piece of pizza.

It's not my bed, though. I'm miles and months away from my real bed in my apartment. This pizza I'm holding is like cardboard, almost inedible. Far from the juicy slices so celebrated in New York that videos of rats carrying it go viral.

And at the end, there's a shot of Lucy, and she's sort of looking at the pizza and she whimpers.

It's not Lucy whimpering, though. It's just a sound effect.

MAY 22, 2020

I have had a new favorite song for a while. "To Live a Life" by First Aid Kit. I like it because there are few songs that describe the kind of loneliness I feel without getting too theatrical or insincere or, at worst, angry. I like this part:

I'm just like my mother
We both love to run . . .
But there is no other way to live a life alone

I like tying this to my mom. My mom is open to dating, but not really. She's open to dinners. Vacations. She wants friends and dogs. She explains to me that it's all a compromise, and she maybe doesn't want to do that at this point in her life. She did that for sixteen years. Her heart was broken. And my mom painfully and with great difficulty moved on. What good is a compromise if you feel you are betraying yourself a little, and *then* you find out it was one-sided the whole time and it turns out people don't actually work on an honor system? I don't blame her.

As I get older, I start looking at my cells basically under a microscope to see where my mother and I overlap. I am afraid we have too many similar genetic sections or whatever that keep us both mistrustful, afraid, self-conscious. We seem to exist in similar loneliness, but somehow my being single is an offense. Hers is, as far as I can tell among people who matter, a strong fabulous choice.

But don't get me wrong. She *is* strong. And smart. Sometimes too clinical/hospital. She's got a sort of compartmentalization you must have to be able to work in health care (which of course stands out to me as a person who went to theater school). But it can feel a little cold sometimes. For instance, when I called her because I needed my mom after the first bad news during Owen's last week, she said, "Shit. He's dying."

"Mama, please," I said. "I know. I can't say it or think it. Not in those words or any. I can't give up on someone who has made it clear he's not giving up."

Remembering her humanity before just being a retired nurse practitioner in crisis mode, she said, "Don't count him out. Go visit him."

Of course, I would never get to visit. I had those sudden, cruel couple of hours.

I think this is one of my biggest takeaways. Not one he taught me, necessarily, but maybe one I just figured out and put into my own words. Owen never showed us he was sad or scared. He could be frustrated, sure. But—and maybe it was because I wasn't his immediate family or his girlfriend—the majority of the time I got to see him, even though the cancer and all the treatments were the elephant in the room, Owen performed a magic trick and he Stephen King "thinner"-ed that damn elephant. His ingenuity and leadership could never be matched. He had stories and laughter and music as his ways of telling us about his experiences, or what he called his "troubles," and that elephant shrank. We always talked about something else for the most part.

I had this question posed to me recently: "How did Owen do it?"

I don't know.

I never asked. Doesn't feel like something to ask. Just to believe.

I think it became pretty clear to me, from the moment my handsome string bean opened his door to me that night for dinner, that a cancer diagnosis, even *brain cancer,* for a person you love, who has made it clear their intention is to "win," can be taken no other way than "YES YOU WILL WIN." Cancer doesn't have rules. Like so many evil things. How do you play in a game where there are no rules and it's unfair and you may not last till the end of the game?

I don't know.

Add it to my pile of questions.

I think the minute someone is given a cancer diagnosis, you stop asking them so many questions. And I'm one for honesty, to my own detriment. So maybe this is a good lesson to learn. You will have questions keep you up at night. You can yell them to an empty room. Write them in a journal. In a book. But you can't ask them.

This is why I can't write Owen's complete story. I only know what he showed me, and I tried not to ever be intrusive, and what he showed me was the most special human on earth.

But maybe . . . if I'm allowing myself to even form the questions in my brain right now, I would want to ask:

What does surgery feel like? What does chemo feel like? Does your head hurt? What do you think will happen to you? Is it okay with you that I'm scared? Do you know I cry about you all the time, mainly because I love you so much, but also because the truth is I'm really scared and I can't say that out loud? Am I allowed to ask you so many questions? This isn't a question, but thank you for coming into my life again. Can I tell you that while I'm maybe not cult-member wide-eyed convinced you'll be okay, I really am sincerely convinced? Because it's you and the alternative is unfathomable. Is that okay to say? Have you ever been scared? I have. How do you get around it? Do you know how very deeply I love you and Leda? And where is the European-detective-show-style whiteboard that I can stand in front of every night like a hotshot, trying to answer the biggest question?

The biggest question is not what you think. It isn't my dad's question: *why* did this happen. Not yet, not to me. I want to know *how*. I want to know how to best look at the fear and uncertainty in your own life, but also in every face around you that loves you and can't hide their sympathy and worry, and not give in. I want to know how to not just say but feel the words you texted at the Knicks/Bulls game:

Psh well not with that attitude you can't.

I'm trying, O. I'm listening for you.

MAY 28, 2020

We have one more week in this house before we have to pack up and move out because another renter booked it for a long-term rental. It's really sad to leave, and I've loved our host, Megan, and appreciated all of the kindness she's shown us, but I also never want to feel like I'm taking advantage or making things more difficult for anyone. I decided I am not ready to go back to my apartment in the city though. Even thinking about the possibility of being in that apartment again brings on a panic and crushing loneliness. So we found a new rental home nearby, in Rhinebeck, and I'll spend more of the summer there. I'm thinking about maybe trying to grow my own lettuce there. Maybe tomatoes. Who knows?

I'm going to try to make it a home.

With this pause in life, I am trying hard not to feel like I'm losing time. It seems a losing thought, but one I keep inching toward. It's not useful thinking and feels ultimately unnecessary. Everyone talks about 2020 like it's the worst year they've ever seen. But they said that about 2016, too. And 2017. I wonder when we will collectively say something is a good year.

Although I'm moving around different rentals

in the Hudson Valley this summer, I do have a house of my own in Los Angeles. I haven't thought about it much. It's been hard. Because it's in California, and I don't know when I'll get there again. I don't know when I'll even get on a plane. Plus, I'm still a bit stubborn about being on the East Coast right now, holding on to some resentment maybe about the way New York was hit so hard and left to drown. How some articles seem to blame New York for the spread. How people didn't believe me at first during those early weeks in March. And I haven't let go of it yet. I'm afraid of not being close to New York, to people who maybe share that sentiment in some way. New York is also where my family lives. Leda is here. Jack is here. I'm afraid if I leave, I won't be able to come back. And I'm not ready for that yet.

So I'm making a temporary home out here, even if that means a couple of different houses and some storage containers. I don't think that's too much of a stretch for me. Even with my LA house, I have split the last couple of years between there and New York. I think I'm comfortable moving around because I never have to feel "stuck." I like wearing different hats. (Or wigs in my case. I have a wig drawer in LA.) I like watching the Michael Jordan documentary and remembering growing up in Chicago, and considering that a part of my identity. I like being able to say I'm someone who made a life in New York. It's a hard city! I like the late nights and the hard work and the fact that everything feels attainable. I can get anything I need delivered to me. I can walk to work. I can get home at five a.m. and order Indian food if I want. Then, I like having a home in LA, where I am a person who can exercise in the yard in the sunshine and eat fresh produce. I make lots of salads. I get flowers delivered once every two weeks. I had a standing "greenery" order where I got palm leaves and bear grass delivered to display in vases around the house. I love bringing up the greenery because I've never been a person who thought about buying leaves for my home, or that the leaves are called greenery. I had to google that when I moved in. I am proud of myself for making a life in both places. But I think I like having both partly because maybe I'm scared to "choose" which person I am. I don't have to quite settle anywhere.

I bought my house in 2017. I had been staying in Airbnbs in LA every summer and liked the change. I enjoyed the homes, but they were never mine. I also felt like my life had become stagnant somehow, not having the milestones other people have to acknowledge growth and progression. I wasn't going to get married any time soon. I wasn't planning on having children soon. And I didn't want that to be something I mourned.

I don't think my life has ever taken a normal trajectory, and I've found that when I embrace "veering off" instead of beating myself up, I am open to unexpected nice things and I am even able to sometimes feel lucky. I got expelled from public school and then dropped out. I wasn't sure I'd graduate high school. But my life didn't end. Instead I found my wonderful art school. I found my joy again. I graduated on time. I met Megu.

I found my house with a wonderful Realtor who held my hand through the whole process. I did a commercial for Triscuit crackers in 2017 and finally felt like I was ready to make a big investment. I wasn't totally financially comfortable, but maybe there'd be more Triscuit commercials in my future, you know? I would make it work. I wanted, really *needed,* my own life milestone. I am not a movie star. I'm not married. I don't have kids. But I have a fucking home!

It's a little midcentury home with exposed beams and a cool spiral staircase and hardwood floors. It's got a 1970s vibe that I love. I don't know that I have a particular aesthetic or style, but if I do, I think it's that. My friend Markus came with me to the open house. It didn't have a big kitchen or bathroom, which are both important to me—a separate bathtub and shower is basically how I would describe the height of luxury—so I wasn't totally sold on it. Markus

154

is a photographer and filmmaker and has much more of an eye for what something *can* be, and he told me I couldn't pass on that house. I could make a kitchen. I could make a bathroom. But the bones of the house were the most important. He was right.

I found an amazing designer named Nicole, and she worked magic and built me my dream home. I have a giant bathtub now. I have ample counter space and an Italian stove! I have banquet seating! I cried when I saw my house all finished. I felt more loved than I had in a long time, if that makes sense.

If you can't tell, I feel disorganized and messy most of the time. I've never really known how to explain who I am. I seem to just keep talking (or writing, in this case) and hoping someone gets a sense of me that way. This designer, Nicole, had many conversations with me, sometimes over margaritas, and she really learned about me better than I think I ever have. Every detail she added in the home felt personal and felt like a gift from someone who not only had figured me out but seemed to celebrate me as well. I don't easily celebrate myself or know how to love myself correctly. I have felt unlovable or unlikable at my lowest. I've felt those lows for years: in grade school, where I sought out other aliens; when my dad walked out and I lost my best friend; when my first love, Henry, and I broke up; when my second love, Michael, left me in 2014, saying I was a "firecracker" and he wanted something more peaceful. (I hear this often from boys I've dated—it's partly why I consider myself a werewolf.)

Nicole designed a home for me that I loved so much and was so proud to show off. It was as if she was showing me the best parts of myself, which are sometimes harder to pinpoint when everything is disorganized. And harder to see because the lows are so much louder than the highs. I'm trying my best these days to give them equal weight.

Thinking about this reminds me of a really special moment my senior year at that art school. I had somehow been allowed into an established group of friends who were all a thousand times cooler than I was. Painters and musicians, real *artists,* who seemed so comfortable with themselves. I always say I think I was the coolest I've ever been when I was eighteen. Because I got to be around these people. One girl, Mary, was a painter with dreadlocks and a nose ring. She dated a friend of mine for a while. We weren't particularly close, as I always felt like I lacked the elegance or grace she seemed to carry naturally. I felt like I was kind of the physical embodiment of Roseanne singing the national anthem—jarring and loud and awkward.

I was shocked when Mary said she had a gift

for me for my birthday. I didn't know she ever thought about me! Her gift was a homemade wallet made of index cards that she'd painted and then laminated with packing tape and stitched together. It was a swirling mix of dark purple and blue and black. I thought it was really really pretty. She wrote a note with the wallet. I can't remember her exact wording but she said something along the lines of, "Sometimes the most beautiful things come from dark places."

I carried that wallet with me for years until it disintegrated finally, as things do.

I realize as much as I've tried not to settle in anywhere, I've let it settle in me that maybe I *am* a monster, a firecracker, too chaotic. Maybe my dark parts, my anger and depression and anxiety, make me impossible to truly love.

But Nicole and Mary saw something else. Something colorful and beautiful even.

Owen and Leda kept showing up for me.

And then Jack. He's still around, isn't he?

So maybe . . .

MAY 30, 2020

My best friend from college, Sam, has a beautiful band with her husband, Jim. The band name is Jim and Sam.

She sends me a couple of songs before they are finished. As soon as I listen to one particular song, "Good on the Other Side," I start weeping.

I tell her how much I liked it.

She says, "Is it weird to say I was thinking of you while writing it? And Jack?"

I cry even more after she says that, although now, looking back, how could I not know?

I listen over and over all night.

See me from my spiraling
If I let you inside
I promise not to hide
The shit in my head
I've got some stuff
But if you can look past it
There's good on the other side

I really do think sometimes people see so much sad in me. More than I imagine is there anyway. But they misname it. They think my loneliness comes from being alone, without a romantic partner. I don't mind that part so much. I have odd moments sometimes where I wonder if seeing me alone hurts my friends more than it hurts me. And why? I feel so proud of the work I've done on my own. And feeling alone is not limited to those of us without partners.

But I am not so closed off.

I am always lightly ready to fall hard, because truly, in my opinion, if you have to fall, fall hard.

But I say all of this wondering if it will ever be a possibility. Will I like someone so much and they like me back enough to stick with me? I know it sounds cliché but I have felt it so much in life. I believe we all leave. Especially the ones who once chose me. They've all left. And I swear I don't mean to be dramatic. But that's what I've known.

I will never be pretty enough.

I will never be relaxed enough.

I will never know how to make someone feel he's home.

I will never fully control this big mouth.

I will never lose my humiliating and unhelpful fear of him leaving.

My dad, my best friend, left our home in 1995 and said one night a week is good from now on; my brother held that axe to the fridge but not me. He wouldn't hurt me. Whose side was I supposed to be on?

All I know is I don't know how to be on my side.

I call myself a werewolf. I hate saying this to anyone.

When I get feelings for someone, I lose control. I can't get rid of it or even quite access it in solo therapy. It's so physical. My brain is the most creative when it comes to how someone can hurt me. I black out. I cry. I have punched my fists into walls. And forgotten the next day. And I'm left so embarrassed. *This pain wasn't meant for you to see! It's mine!*

I scare people. And I should, I think.

Owen and Leda cheered for me and still do. Not because they think I'm in need. But because they recognize something I don't. They love me with glassy eyes, the older cousin, as if I'm Michael fucking Jordan! (I am very much not MJ.)

Can I stop scaring people? Can I stop feeling like any second I will be left?

Now what?

This is one I'm having a harder time with, O. Navigating my path to feeling okay alone. Or navigating my life to a comfortable place if I'm attempting "not alone."

You did it so well. You did it with cancer. You did it with panache!

Girls still write me about you.

But you are Owen and I am me.

So I hold my Owen compass up to my sky, to my head, to my heart, and try to figure out how the hell he did it.

And tonight I just break down because WHY COULDN'T I HAVE ASKED YOU MORE WHEN YOU WERE HERE?

It's fruitless. It's stupid. I know. I just needed to let go of one more thought.

I love you, O, and I'll keep waiting on sunny days and birdsong and knowing that's maybe enough for a day.

JUNE 1, 2020

Matt has decided to move back into his apartment in Brooklyn. It's sad to see him go, but I think he misses his things, like his own bed. Those little comforts are so important right now. He isn't far away though, since driving is now the only form of travel that feels safe—Los Angeles may as well be in outer space at this point—and we let him know that he's always welcome back (following a quarantine and negative test).

Our friends Tommy and Shawn come up to visit. They live in New York with Tommy's mother, who has preexisting conditions, so they've been very careful. They get tested often. Tommy especially seems to be as crazy as I am about monitoring COVID news. So I feel comfortable with them visiting, entering my bubble.

It's the most I've laughed in months I think. We went to a small local farm and I bought lettuce plants and a tomato plant. We drove there in a convertible they'd rented for the drive up to see us. What a gift: driving through windy country roads surrounded by green. I wore my mask on my head to control my hair like Thelma and Louise. I took out my phone for a minute to take a video.

I remember a snippet of a video played at Owen's service. I remember watching it in Ed and Laurel's apartment, actually, wearing earbuds and sitting in front of a laptop with Ed over my shoulder. He'd asked if I wanted to see the video montages Owen's friend had been putting together. I had done such a good job of not breaking down in front of them and I knew I would not be able to hold it in if I watched. But I couldn't say no, and I think it was okay, even though I wanted so much to be the strong funny one for them, knowing the trauma they had just gone through during that last week. Not even a week. It was faster than that. I don't like thinking about it.

My hands shook as I watched the video, sitting in that room, in the heaviest silence because Owen wasn't there speaking loudly, and it was hard for anyone else to speak for a while because of the shock. And if you start speaking, what's the first thing you'll say? Where does your story go now? Are you ready to acknowledge this horror? How?

I was holding a tissue Ed handed to me at the start. My body shook the way it had that day on my bed in California. It was hard to breathe. In those moments, it's like my body does not want to take another breath because it's so painful, so I exhale and shake until I'm forced to gasp for another breath.

Owen's face came on the screen. And it hurt so much, as it does today when I picture him. He's smiling. He smiled a lot. He has a really great smile. But as I watch, I'm seeing so many parts of his life I didn't share with him. I didn't know he was so dizzy so often, and would lie on the couch on his back, looking up. There were a lot of shots that started this way: Owen looking introspective maybe. Then someone would say something, he'd notice, and he'd instantly grin. Without fail.

Then Ed says, "This is my favorite: the dudes in a convertible." Owen is in the backseat of a convertible and his friend is taking a video. They are listening to "Pretty Woman." There is a bit of silly self-indulgence like any selfie video and they are certainly cool-looking dudes. But Owen is less concerned about being cool. He's smiling again, his auburn hair blowing in the wind. He's really happy. He's just cruising with friends and letting it feel good.

I felt good in the car, at first, but I noticed on the way home that I was holding my breath. My chest was tight. I am still so full of anxiety about being out, about driving, about being among other people in any way, about leaving the safety of this house. I worry there won't be emergency services if we get hurt. I worry other drivers are less careful because there are fewer cars on the road. I worry about deer jumping out in front of us. I worry about windy turns and small bridges. I start really noticing a weird intersection: "Oh, I guess we don't have a stop sign, only them. That seems confusing." I try to keep the panic out of my voice. When I notice my chest is tight, I wonder if I got COVID just now from touching fruit at the produce stand. Did I just ruin everything? I'm so relieved when we get home. But I don't say it out loud. I smile and say thank you and run in to see Lucy.

I wonder how long it will feel this way. I wonder if someday I can just cruise, like you did, not scared, listening to "Pretty Woman." Making your dad smile as he watched you, even during impossible grief.

I wonder what Owen was thinking in those videos when he's just looking up. Is he ever anxious? Is he curious about where he will go?

But he doesn't stay there. He always comes back.

"Hey, Owen."

And he turns to the person with the camera, and immediately he grins.

At the end of the night, we laugh hard in a way I really needed. We are wearing wigs and watching that new show about ball culture on HBO Max, *Legendary*. We cheer for the House of Balmain tonight. We've had wine and my favorite pasta and salad. We get a little high from this

"Unicorn Dust" edible that Tommy and Shawn brought. I start walking the room in my blond hair and I say that I am "Jennifer Convertibles of the House of Convertibles." The boys become Keevin Convertibles, Sharmy Convertibles, and Monchichi Convertibles. I stay up until one thirty or something, much later than I've been staying up these past couple of months, and I'm laughing so hard the whole time. I stop for a second every now and then, wondering if there's something I should be worried about. But I let it go, I'm fine, and I let myself just laugh. And I just keep laughing. It feels so good.

Maybe that's how I can cruise for now.

JUNE 2, 2020

People are reaching out to their exes; so says the *New York Times*. This is not true for me. I can't.

Yours is not the only story I don't know how to tell, O.

I always say I have two exes that really mattered in my life. I've dated plenty, enough for a lifetime maybe. Not because I'm a person who seeks it out. I don't. I'm actually very comfortable being single. I just enjoy any kind of adventure, maybe. And as I said, I like to smooch. Sometimes I play a dumb game with myself and try to see if I can remember and write down all the names that have drifted in and then out of my life. I had my first real boyfriend, although it was brief, when I was fifteen. It's been over twenty years going in and out of companionship. It's just another home I haven't quite found.

My first real love is a hard story to tell because it's heavy. For many different reasons. And I can't tell it like a normal story where there is a fixed morality and therefore good guys and bad guys. I don't want you to hate him. I don't want you to hate me. I don't know if I'm allowed to take that stance without feeling like I'm letting people down.

I might have to bounce around this one, too. I won't tell you everything. Some of it doesn't feel like my story to tell. So here are parts, because it's easier that way.

The beginning:

I'm fifteen and I'm sitting outside on a lunch break at my public school with my friend Alex. (I'm changing her name because after we lost touch later in life, I heard she struggled with mental illness and joined a very strict cultlike church and cut everyone out. Maybe this detail isn't important, but I think it is pretty sad and just another example of how many ways we lose people in life.) I'm a sophomore. I don't know it yet, but I'm going to be expelled right before spring. We notice a boy I know from chorus, Adam, sitting across the way. He's a tall, friendly, goofy guy with messy curly blond hair. He's sitting with a boy I don't know.

"Oh, that's Henry," Alex says. "He was really popular in my junior high school. All the girls thought he was cute." Well, that certainly piques my interest. I try to get a better glimpse of Henry. Okay, he is very handsome. He's got a big smile and long eyelashes and dark hair and caramel skin. He and Adam are looking over at us, laughing with each other. Alex and I look back and maybe yell some dumb teen flirty thing out like, "What are you laughing at?" Adam motions that he will tell me later. Yes, he will. I'll bring it up casually if he doesn't, pretending it's not all I'm thinking about all day.

"The guy I'm with said you were pleasant to look at."

I find out we have mutual friends. I find out everything I can about him, obviously. He's half Indian. He wears Adidas. He's a year ahead of me. He used to live in the wealthy town next to mine, but now he lives in Oak Park. We hang out with friends a couple nights. He and I sneak glances at each other often.

I am at my friend Liz's house one night. I sleep over there all the time. Her family jokingly calls me "the other sister." Liz and I are really close, joined at the hip. She's a year older and drives us around for hours some nights as we sing along with the radio and smoke cigarettes. She's the best singer I know. We had a million inside jokes that I can't quite remember and won't ever get to laugh about with her again as Liz passed away from a heroin overdose in 2015. I didn't even know she had been using.

Liz and I talk about boys a lot. She has a crush on Adam. I have a huge crush on Henry. We call Adam on her landline, heads together so we can both hear the speaker. We look up Henry's number. I call him, somehow. Liz and I are giggling. We make plans to hang out on our own. Oh my God.

He drives his mom's little black BMW. It has a police scanner that is constantly making bizarre sounds and lighting up. He says it's a common

169

feature in that type of car. I believe anything and everything he says. We drive around one night, going anywhere but home. At one point we pull over. I keep saying, "Well, what do *you* want to do?" And he says, "I don't know, what do *you* want to do?" We are both shy but somehow not too shy, because here we are, in this car together, alone finally. He exhales and looks out the front window. He says, "Actually there is something I've wanted to do for a while." He turns to me. "And that's kiss you." I think I managed an "Okay" before we were kissing. I feel like fainting. He's good at making me swoon.

Some nights we talk on the phone for hours, until my mom yells at me that it's time for bed. We start making secret plans, and it becomes a regular occurrence for Henry to drive over around midnight so I can sneak him into my living room. We kiss and sometimes I just lie in his arms, in the dark in my living room, hoping my mom won't wake up. He usually leaves after an hour or so. He seems to want to be around me as much as I want to be around him.

Months later, we are driving around again, daring each other to "say something mushy." I'm driving now. Around and around but neither of us is saying it. The letters I've slowly traced on his back for weeks now, while we lay next to each other, wondering if he'd be able to read my secret message: "I-L-O-V-E-Y-O-U." I decide neither of us is going to be brave enough to say it. I take us back to my house and park in the garage. We walk out of the door together, and he stops me. We are standing right where I saw my mom and dad five years earlier the day they came home to tell me they were separating. My back is against the door. He says, "I don't know if I have anything mushy to say, but I can tell you that I'm in love with you." I say, "Me too," and then "I have to sit down." Due to my vasovagal fainting thing, I'm going to pass out. But I am so happy.

A year or so later we are in this same spot. I'm crying hard. He's been drinking and he's yelling at me. Loud. Mean. He slams his hands into the door. I'm sobbing and I go inside. Not long after, the doorbell rings. I look through the glass puffy eyed, still crying. It's my neighbor. He won't stop pounding on the door. Finally, I open it up. His son thought he saw a man hit me. Am I okay? I assure him I'm okay. I just got in a fight with my boyfriend. I promise I'm okay.

He goes to the University of Michigan in Ann Arbor for college. He's really smart and a great writer. He writes stories about us. He will do this for years. He always uses the names "Henry" and "Sophie." I'm doing the same now.

He doesn't stay long at school. He leaves. He stays between my house and his parents' apartment. We spend weekends in the summer at his beautiful home in Union Pier, Michigan. His family takes me on vacations I never dreamed of, to Florence and Rome and Seville. We dip bread in bright green olive oil from Umbria while sitting at a restaurant in the Piazza Navona. He takes me to what will become my favorite place to visit, La Carbonería, a flamenco bar in Seville. I will follow him anywhere.

He lives with me and friends in a tiny apartment my first year of college at CalArts. I'm nervous when we go out. He's gotten even worse with drinking. He drinks a case of beer one night and I cancel our plans to go out with friends. He's got that look on his face where I know he's not there. My good friend Markus is visiting. Everyone just kind of ignores Henry because he's rambling and rolling cigarettes and playing his music loudly and laughing with us as if we are all having a great time. Then he decides he's mad. He grabs a coffeepot that isn't quite empty and he walks over and throws it at me. The hot coffee burns my chest. I go into the bathroom and quickly take my shirt off to get it off my skin and look to see if I'm burned. He storms into the bathroom, knocking over a glass that shatters on the ground. He pushes me down, almost choking me, on the broken glass. I have never done this before, but I'm scared, so I yell for Markus and my roommate Alex. They both run in and pull Henry off me. I quickly grab a towel. I'm not wearing a shirt and I'm so humiliated. Henry leaves and

Alex locks the door behind him. Both he and Markus ask if I'm okay. None of us know what to say or do.

Later that night, I open the door so he has a place to stay. We spend the morning with him crying in my arms. He's so sorry and he's such a monster. I should never forgive him. But I do. I love him so much. He's the gentlest person I know when he isn't this way. We know everything about each other. He loves me as completely as I love him.

We break up a bunch of times over the years. We call it final after a doomed vacation back to Spain and Italy right after I finish the run of a show I did my last year at school. We got to perform and tour France for five weeks. Henry meets me and we break up after fighting the whole time. I do not miss the irony of visiting the Italian ruins with him.

I move to Los Angeles that summer and move in with Markus and my friend Cindy. I'm going to try to make it work in LA. Isn't that what I'm supposed to do as an actor? I start to see someone I work with for a month or two that fall. He is older. He rides a motorcycle. He spends all of the tips he's earned to take me to nice dinners. I think he's sort of a fun bad boy. Then I realize he drinks a lot, doesn't he? And one night he cuts his hand at work and I'm bandaging him up, realizing I don't want this again. I don't tell anybody at work that we were starting to date. I just break it off with him. I don't feel like a nice person.

Then, slowly, Henry and I start talking again. By January he's living in the house with Markus, Cindy, and me. I'm so happy to have him back. We cry in each other's arms about how much we missed each other. I love him so much. I told him about seeing someone else, before we decided to try again. He seemed like a different person. He said he understood.

"Did you fuck him?" He throws a glass of wine at my wall. It ruins the flamenco poster I have hanging. I got it in Seville. It's a similar image to the ones his parents had framed in their gorgeous apartment. It's really the only thing I have in my room. I don't have much money. I make $9 an hour selling wine at a deli five nights a week. I'm not sure I'm cut out for LA.

Another night I wake up to Henry crying. He's on the internet. I think he's watching porn. He says, "You did that with someone else." He's got a knife to his arm. He's carving letters onto his skin. He says he's writing "covet nothing." I think of the letters I traced lightly on his back. I hate how much I've hurt him.

One morning I run out of my door, terrified, to find Henry, who is getting something from his pickup. "I'm pregnant, Henry."

I leave Los Angeles after only seven months

174

with all my things piled in Henry's truck. I'm twenty-three. I'm not pregnant anymore when we leave.

Not long after we return to Chicago, we split up again. He moves to Northern California to live with his aunt and uncle. His aunt is a really outspoken and funny teacher. His uncle is an arborist and built his own house. He's Henry's hero.

I'm working at a restaurant now called the Pasta Shoppe and living in my old house with my mom. I'm a server. I'm not great at it but I went to art school to be an actor. I'm not sure what else I'm supposed to do. I'm taking classes at the Second City. I recently quit smoking. It's only been a couple of months since Henry left. This day I am working the Sunday shift, my favorite because it's a daytime shift and you get to be outdoors and usually there are enough customers to make a decent amount of tips. My cell phone starts buzzing about halfway through. I see that it's Cindy calling. She leaves a message. I check it on a break.

"Hey, Cecily, sorry to bug you but I just got a call from a hospital in Palo Alto. They said this was the last number called in a phone for an unidentified person they found after he was hit by a train. I'm not sure what's happening. Is Henry okay?"

I run outside after telling my boss I have an

emergency. I can't think straight. I'm panicking. I call Henry. No answer. I call my parents. My dad and stepmom pick me up. They calm me down a little and I call Henry's mom. I'm so scared. He was hit by a train. His mom answers, "Oh, Cecily." She's crying but not sobbing. She says she doesn't know exactly what happened yet. I ask about head injuries. She says she doesn't think so. He's alive, but he's not awake. They are flying to California tomorrow. Henry's brother is there now.

I spend that night smoking again with Henry's best friend. We decide we should fly to California, too. I don't have the money, but I use my new credit card to get a ticket on Southwest.

He's at Stanford. He's in an induced coma. They had to amputate his entire left leg. He's had an operation and his stomach is held together with staples. They are worried about infection. His brother is a doctor. He assures us it's the best trauma center in the world. Henry will be okay.

I walk in circles endlessly around the hospital. I'm worried about Henry. I wonder if I should be there. Will he want to see me when he wakes up? I've never felt so confused. In a day or two, his dad says they want to bring him out of the coma now. Will I see if I can wake him up? I go into his room. I hold his hand. I try not to look at the awful bandage on his upper thigh, where his leg used to be. It smells like disinfectant, but there

176

is another terrible smell and I think it is his flesh and blood. His long eyelashes flutter as I talk to him. I think he squeezes my hand. He doesn't wake up though.

A couple hours later, the nurses say he's up. He's out of it though. They decide his brother will be the one who first tells him he lost his leg. I'm allowed in later, with Henry's best friend. He smiles at me. "Hey. I'm glad you're here." I immediately cry. He says, "Come here," and we hug. And he kisses me. We spend an hour or so that day making light jokes and listening to his music.

I fly back and forth every couple of weeks while Henry is in the hospital. I max out my credit card. But I need to be there with him. He has this amazing nurse who tells me it's great that I'm there. He thinks I'm really helping Henry heal. I sleep on chairs next to him. I stroke his hand. He sometimes reaches for me. He's nicer to me than he's been in years.

Later I hear that some of the hospital staff thought he was such a romantic after they went through his journal trying to learn his identity. He had written all about his "girl." I knew it wasn't me. I don't bring it up with him. I can't think about anything except today.

I could write more, as there are years of back-and-forth with Henry. But it's all the same story, just different details. So many memories I keep locked up. We could never end up together and we could never quite let each other go.

It's a hard story to tell, you know? I loved him so much, he loved me, maybe part of us always will. But it's a painful and shameful story, too, and one I can't share easily because the only responsible "moral" way to think of it means I have to denounce it all. And I tried for years. But I can't today.

He visited me once in New York. I tried to be distant and friendly with him and keep things civil. He was nice, not seeming to expect anything physical with me. We talked about his niece. The night before he was going to leave, I woke up in a panic. What was I doing? What if I never saw him again? I went to him asleep on my couch. I crawled next to him and he kissed me again and we were both sort of desperate for one another that night.

It always ends the same, though, so I don't see him anymore. I can't. I am older now. I don't want love like that, and I know that as a concrete truth. But I'm still glad I had it. I don't know if it makes me lucky or unlucky. I don't know if I'm a bad person. I just know that in order to remember the days of tracing letters on his back and feeling so lightheaded because I loved him so much, I have to also remember the cruelty and feeling lower than I ever had. I cannot separate them. And it's all painful in some way. Part of me

178

worries that someday I will get a call and learn that he's gone.

So I leave things with him as two people living on clouds, and every now and then, if our clouds pass by, we can wave.

There is a person out there who has loved me more than anyone and I've loved him more than anyone. But he is just a person out there. And that's how our story has to end.

JUNE 3, 2020

I tried to write a chapter about my first love, the person I was with off and on for seven years, starting at fifteen. I tried hard to figure out how to talk around certain things but still be honest. It's a huge and heavy part of my life. I tried to include as much of the good as the bad, which is what you do when living in a toxic relationship anyway.

I think it's important in knowing who I am and why I have such a tough time with relationships. So I emailed him a copy. Partly because I thought it was sweet in many ways, and partly to make sure he was okay with it, but I wasn't too worried. I left a lot out and didn't use his name.

But he doesn't want me to talk about it publicly, even with a fake name. "You must realize this will be my entire public presence. I can't tell you what to do, or what your story is, or how to tell it. But I would never dream of talking about you, your life, or us publicly. Not only because you've always guarded your privacy tightly and actively feared that I might reveal things about you. Also because public discourse is dangerous, fragmented and intractable, and I could never control how the slightest detail might be digested and interpreted about you in the storm of public perception."

He's embarrassed about the things he did to me. So I can't talk about them.

They still happened, though. Even if you don't talk about it.

I'm shaken by that interchange. Still shaken today.

I feel really low about it. I'm confused.

For years I lived this way. Because I was embarrassed, too.

I accepted a lot. I'm not proud. But I think the secrecy and shame are part of why you get stuck in really bad places.

In an abusive relationship.

So here are empty pages. There should be eleven.

"Thanks for understanding. Good luck with your project."

JUNE 7, 2020

The world stopped. It stopped for some months, hesitating, not sure what would happen next. When we stopped, every sound made became amplified. And we all heard the sound of a man saying that terrible three-word refrain: "I can't breathe." George Floyd was suffocated by three police officers on his body, one with a knee on his neck for almost nine minutes. And then this pause, this space, finally provided room for voices that never seem to get to be heard to say, "ENOUGH!" And it is powerful. But it is just the first step, and there is so much work to do to start fixing all the systems that have enabled oppression of Black Americans for years and years. And anger is rarely patient, you know?

JUNE 8, 2020

Dear Jack,

Can you believe it? I finally got to see you again yesterday! It had been eighty-nine days since I last saw you. Some days I wasn't sure I'd ever see you again. Some days, it was all I could think about. Some days, it was all I wanted.

It feels almost unreal. Like I'd been granted one wish for a day and I wished to see you again. Or Cinderella with that midnight curfew when it all disappears. And there you were: Taller than I remembered. Longer hair, glasses, new freckles. No more tailored Italian suits from eBay. Dressed down. And standing in my kitchen in the new house in Hudson!

We went to get wine and I asked you in the car if we had hugged hello. Isn't that funny? I didn't remember. I'm so nervous around you still and I think maybe I worry if I touch you, my hand will go through you, breaking the illusion. You're a bit like my Eurydice this way—and so I'm trying to follow the rules Orpheus couldn't.

We have dinner. I'm barely awake, barely here. It isn't my best showing. I go to bed thinking that I've lost you again.

But in the morning, I get to start over. I'm not

so tired anymore. I'm not so scared. We laze away the day playing my card games: Anomia, Monikers. We sit outside and talk about our families and our jobs and each other. I feel I'm on borrowed time with you but I don't mind, because it's worth any trade: to lie in the sun with my legs draped over you and we talk the way we used to talk. I like talking to you so much. We are good at that. Not great at plenty of other things, but really good at talking to one another.

You thank me for putting up with you. I don't think I put up with you, but I understand feeling that way. I've always struggled with dating and relationships. I've drawn such a clear picture of why it cannot work that it's the chalk door in the movie *Beetlejuice* and it's a real door now. I keep talking about being a werewolf. I hate how quickly I panic that I am being left. *Is today the day?* I fill in every blank space with a bad thought, so I desperately beg for answers each time there's a pause. I have never been sure what to do with my monster. It's ruined so much. At least that's what I've concluded. It's been my narrative.

I read a poem once about demons dancing together: we can love each other because our demons can dance together. I hate that poem. I don't want to throw a party for my demons and I don't want my demons to choose who I get to love. And two demons in love is not the relationship I want. I have been there. When I was Sophie and Henry.

But then there's you, Jack. And you seem to be able to forgive me without even knowing how precious a gift that is to me. And maybe this is how I handle my demons. You don't dance with them, they don't scare you away. You forgive them. You keep talking to me. You're the one guy who knows you put out an oil fire with baking soda or salt, not water. And so I feel so grateful to you.

Thanks for putting up with me.

You left in your grandmother's old car, a Lexus you call "Sexy Lexy," just like the name of a show I tried to make years ago. I've already drawn that constellation for myself. You say it's a new chapter. And I like that. New chapter.

I sat on the steps with Lucy as you drove away, waving your arm out of your window. You're a person who does that.

I thought I'd feel so sad when you left. But instead I feel hopeful. The rest of the day Kevin and I giggle about anything and everything. Everything feels like a victory. There's a Thai restaurant in this town! We figured out Apple TV! The new season of *Drag Race All Stars* has started! A reservation was canceled, so we get to stay in this home through August! So many wins.

It's a new chapter, Jack. Like you said.

And I'll see you soon.

JUNE 14, 2020

Today is the first day I wonder whether the ending to this story might be happy. And I don't even want to say it out loud, but wouldn't it be amazing, after all of these days in isolation trying to find magic and trying to learn how to grieve Owen and grieve Hal and just plain grieve; after all these days with nothing to take up the space around me, leaving room for all the ghosts from my life to stop by for a while, making it so I'd have to look at them; after all these days of rain where I looked for any sunshine because it's what Owen would have done—if maybe I get a happy ending? I have Kevin, I have Lucy, and now I have Jack again. And it's the least alone I've felt in a long time.

I'm still so sad, and I cried in the car today listening to "Perfect Day." I just wanted to listen because it's a song I love. It was my song once, but now I see it has to belong to Hal for a while. Maybe forever. And that grief is attached to the heaviest fucking anchor of COVID and quarantine and police brutality and those awful two weeks in my apartment and that awful week in January. They are all mashed together now, I think. And all of it could easily swallow me someday. But I'm alive. I'm living with it. I am living without Owen and living with everything that means.

So I suppose I could say my happy ending is relative.

But then I can see Owen so clearly, and he would say. "Fuck that, Cec. It's a happy ending!"

And so that's what it will be.

JUNE 21, 2020

This year started with one of the hardest weeks of my life. And I'm just one of many who are still trying to understand how to live with the colossal loss of one of the most wonderful people I've ever met in my life, who happens to be my cousin as well. Owen. My dad's only nephew, who shared his passion for music.

My dad was the one who called me and told me what was happening with my amazing cousin that day, and we cried together on the phone. We spoke side by side at the service. I don't know if I ever remember wanting a hug from my dad so much since I was a little kid and my mom would threaten, "Wait till Dad finds out," but I knew it was an empty threat because nine times out of ten my dad would just give me a huge hug instead of some imaginary admonishment, because we were best friends.

We lost our way a bit in the middle, but we made it back to here. I wait for one very important text after every live show on Saturday: my dad's summary, always far too complimentary of me. I am sorry for the year, and I miss you, Dad. But I'm so thankful for my first best friend who took me on trips to New York often, just the two of us, to see the Broadway shows Uncle Ed produced, because that's what I wanted to do, too! And every time I also got to spend time with my funny little cousins and my funny grandma with the Southern accent and Jackie O hair who called me Lulu and told me my favorite stories as a kid. Like when her sister Jessie fell in a port-o-potty. Or when her brother Alan—nicknamed Pooh— wanted to be a dog playing dress-up with her as kids but she wanted him to be a ballerina and she's the oldest, so there was a picture of Pooh in a tutu chained to a doghouse.

I love you so much, Dad. It isn't easy to say "happy" Father's Day this year, but I know how happy I am that you are my father.

Happy Father's Day to the person I needed to lean on at Owen's service. Happy Father's Day to the big hug I needed most that day we all met to say goodbye and celebrate our boy who loved birds. The big hug that I needed most as a little girl crying in my bedroom because I'd gotten in trouble. My dad.

JUNE 22, 2020

I sent my dad that Father's Day bit and he texted me late last night:

What a Father's Day gift! What a gift, period! Your words mean so, so much to me, girlie. Too momentous to set off tears (at least on first reading). It just made me reflect on how lucky I am to have you in my life and share truth, love, and laughter with you.

We were always best friends and will be forever. We made it through the rough passage of divorce to this place. It's a really good place, even if we don't get to see each other much.

JULY 7, 2020

I want to tell you about one of the most important and special people in my life: my little sister Rashida.

She's not biologically my little sister. She's the little sister the universe gave me.

I met her through friends in Chicago. I saw her Facebook and saw this fired-up activist who mentored kids and was a superhero about helping the world become a better place—but who was also hilarious and silly and one of those people (like my brother) who can't help but start to smile when they talk to you no matter what they are saying. The ones who have a hard time lying because their faces immediately give them away. Probably not great poker players.

One night in Chicago a couple years ago Rashida and I were in a hotel room playing Connect Four. We were participating in a twenty-four-hour comedy and music fundraiser our friend Heather puts together yearly as a way to raise money and gifts to be delivered to families around Chicago on Christmas. I got to go help deliver once. I was humbled to get to be any part of that day, but the thing that stays with me just as much is how many of these homes saw us as a possible threat. Mainly white people showing up at your door. Sometimes we could tell there was an adult hiding in the house because they might have been undocumented. We were there with money and gifts, but these families lived a life where any day the group of mainly white people at the door could be there to take a family member away.

Rashida and I were taking a break from the show and back at the hotel to have a drink and hang out. We played Connect Four because Rashida was determined to beat me finally. This is part of the big sister/little sister relationship. She's never gonna beat me in Connect Four. She'd have three in a row and I'd pretend to not notice and she couldn't help but start to smile and get excited (bad poker player, see?) because she thought she was about to win. I liked to pretend to almost drop my disk and then switch at the last minute to block her move. I am a nerd who does all kinds of puzzles, numbers and words, every day. Of course I'm gonna win! And in the same vein, my grandmother "Dear," my mom's stepmom, could beat me every time. She's a big-time puzzle fan too. She and I each have a subscription to *Games* magazine.

Actually, while we are on the subject, I have to fess up to Rashida here. She used to always take my iPad to play solitaire. Now, I don't judge the solitaire. I use my iPad for puzzles 90 percent of the time. Then she started hiding it from me as a little-sister prank. She'd pretend not to know where it was and that smile would start to show, totally giving her away. One night, I woke up in the middle of the night and went to my living room to see if Rashida had done her prank. I went to one of her two hiding spots, under the chair that once belonged to my landlord Howard. There was my iPad, of course. I took it and hid it deep at the bottom of a basket full of who knows what on a high shelf in my closet. Then I went back to bed. In the morning I went through the moves of pretending to look for my iPad and then giving in.

"Okay, sis, where is it?"

She smiled, so proud of herself, and pretended she didn't know. We played this little game for a couple more minutes until I finally said something like, "It better not be under the chair." Rashida was about to burst. I looked under the chair and said, "Okay, where is it?"

Her face dropped as she realized it wasn't there. "Wait, where is it?"

I pretended we were still playing the game, but Rashida knew that was where she'd left it, so the game took a turn. She immediately suspected I'd moved it. I pretended to suspect her too. Normally, I'm a horrible liar. But when it comes to lies that don't matter, I can be frighteningly good. I sometimes wonder if this makes me slightly sociopathic. I kept making her swear she hadn't taken it, as if I really didn't trust she wasn't playing the game anymore. She promised me over and over she put it under the chair and hadn't moved it again. Neither of us knew what had happened. I pretended to be stressed that it was just gone. Then I did what I would have done in that situation and sort of shrugged in defeat like, "Well, nothing I can do. I just have to accept that it's gone." She kept looking, of course.

I waited a week and then texted her that I found it under my bed.

Are you sure you didn't hide it there and forgot? I swear I don't remember putting it there.

I've never come clean with her about this until now, and she never hid my iPad again.

Anyway, we are playing Connect Four over and over and I win every time. This is not really a brag on my part. My love for puzzles isn't quite "cool," and I remember I used to hide every *Games* magazine frantically if a boy was ever coming to my house. God forbid he find out I like crossword puzzles and sudoku-style puzzles. He might realize I'm not the supercool badass he thought I was.

At one point we laugh about something or another, and I realize I used to laugh this way with my old best friend from junior high and high school, Liz. And I look up at Rashida and I say, "I really wish you could've met Liz. I think we would all have had a lot of fun." She says, "Me too, sis."

About two months earlier I got a Facebook message from Liz's sister Laura. I assumed it was a funny video that would make the three of us, and probably *only* the three of us, laugh so hard we'd cry. But it wasn't that.

"We lost our Lizzie today."

I had and still do have a really hard time with this one. We were joined at the hip for those years. How did I end up here and somehow she's gone? We had fallen out of touch a bit, but when we talked we easily and immediately fell right back into the silly secretive world we had created over countless sleepovers, or the sing-alongs we'd have driving around aimlessly in her dad's red car, or all the times we cheated playing Spades with friends by passing secret signals to each other (we were always partners of course). If we touched our forehead with our right hand, we had the ace. Nose, we had the queen. Chin: jack.

I remember telling people this on that Sunday I flew back to Chicago after a show, my foot in a boot after breaking it on vacation in Spain right before going back to work. We didn't have her body for the service because the county hadn't released it. My friend was "evidence" still. So we spoke in front of many pictures of her, and although it was hard, I knew wherever she was, if I didn't speak she would dramatically show her disapproval. I loved how dramatic she could be. She was also the best singer I knew, and everybody spoke about her voice at the service. But I wanted them to also know how funny she was. How much time I spent laughing so hard with Liz and Laura. She was fucking hilarious. I had a surreal moment where these sweet people we knew in high school came up to me to say how sorry they were, as they knew how close we'd been. And I sincerely thanked them even though in my head all I wanted to do was say, "You're being so kind, but Liz and I definitely used to laugh together about something weird you did that we found hilarious," and then laugh through tears about how bizarre it is to be consoled by them while simultaneously thinking of the weird thing about them that used to crack Liz and me up.

The hardest part for me, I think, or at least for now until some new phase of grief takes over, is that I have so many inside jokes that I can't quite remember, and the only person who knew the other part of the joke isn't there anymore. We had so much just between us two chickens. And those laughs were precious to me. Those jokes and secrets made up the majority of my life at thirteen, fourteen, fifteen. It felt like those years went when Liz went. It still feels that way.

And that day in that hotel room with Rashida, I realized I was again having a slumber party and sneaking off with my best friend because we had the most fun just the two of us—laughing and shit-talking. And it felt like a gift.

I like to think the universe brought Rashida into my life as a way to help me grieve my friend, because Rashida was a reminder of all of my favorite parts of that friendship. And it was nice to think of those moments and think of Liz that way.

And Rashida and I realized I was also brought into her life for a reason. Because of how quickly I became her older sister and she fell into the role of little sister just as fast.

Rashida lost her oldest brother when she was a kid. She has other siblings, but their relationship was different. The way she talks about him now, you see the admiration she feels for him. And she lost him in such a painful way.

She grew up on the South Side of Chicago. The city didn't have a trauma center on the South Side at the time, despite the fact that a huge number of people lived there. So when an ambulance came for him, there was nowhere close by to take him. Because there wasn't a fucking trauma center.

Our city failed Rashida and her brother and her mother. I grew up outside of the city in Oak Park. I've always known about the racial segregation in Chicago, of course, and I knew the city had seemed to have forgotten about huge neighborhoods. But as a white person from Oak Park, I had never truly felt what that meant. And

I don't mean to say that I do now. But I know Rashida and her family have lived with not only an insurmountable grief, but also the horrible unfairness of systemic racism that is very much a part of what happened to her hero, her big brother. Why was it okay with all of us to ignore these parts of our city? And it is part of what motivated Rashida to become fiercely protective and care about her community, because she's experienced a world that doesn't seem to care about her community much, and so she's had to do it herself.

I say all of this only as a friend admiring the strength and superhero powers of my friend. It is not my story to tell. My story involves Rashida in so many ways, and I'm forever thankful she came into my life. I could go on and on about what an amazing person she is. She volunteered as a mentor for kids on the South Side for years. I say "volunteered" because although it started as a paid position, as in so many other cities and neighborhoods and school districts, funding was slashed and there was no longer money for her work. But that didn't stop her. She worked a night job at Second City and paid for her own transportation and materials and everything you could think of to remain an amazing mentor to these kids. I've had the honor of getting to meet a couple of her mentees, who have gone on to college to pursue business degrees and art degrees and writing degrees and filmmaking degrees, and I'm even more proud to know my friend, who tried to do what she could to make sure these kids had a more equal opportunity to reach their potential because the city (and the country) was not safeguarding that opportunity the same way they do for other kids. And isn't that pretty damn important?

Thank you, Rashida.

She and I used to joke because she said Owen was the first white boy she had a crush on. I told you, the girls love him! My little cousin Leda and Rashida became good friends over the last couple of years. Leda was a teacher and mentor to kids before going back to school to get her master's degree in sports management. That's the other reason Rashida and Leda are so close: those two can talk basketball for *hours*. I like basketball, but they *really* like basketball. They text each other about draft rumors or ESPN alerts and a million other things I'll never understand at that level.

Rashida was there with me in California that awful day in January. I knew she wanted so badly to do anything. I could hear her crying downstairs. She's my family too. Owen is her family too.

She came to the beautiful service. I was glad not only for me but also for Leda, since I know how much Leda loves Rashida. But there was never a question. It's Rashida. Of course she'd be there.

She also flew in when my dad told me about the diagnosis. She wanted to be here with us. I was so grateful to my little sis and got her a first-class ticket for the trip. On her way home after coming to be with my family, the flight attendant stopped her from boarding with the other first-class passengers. She pulled Rashida out of the line to double-check her ticket was really hers and really first-class. Rashida called me from the plane crying. She was embarrassed. Out of the blue, for no reason except she's Black. It was another instance when I felt a fraction of what the statistics and numbers and systemic problems really translate into in real life. It's beyond just "unfair." It's painful. It's humiliating, exhausting, and just really painful.

We talked together, and with her permission, I tried to help in some way at least with the flight. We were able to get her a refund and some baggage perks or something. Later we found out the employee was fired. And while there were some real attempts at righting a wrong in that situation, I'm well aware that it's just one time out of many similar situations for Rashida. So although I'm glad it was dealt with, there have been and will be so many others that will not be dealt with.

I've been out here in the Hudson Valley—

Rhinebeck now—and I am starting to feel okay. Having happy days. Burying my head in the sand by living in my sanctuary in the woods. I know how lucky I am.

Then last week Rashida texted me.

My 18 year old niece was found dead after she didn't return home last night. I gotta get home. just letting you know. cause I'm fucked up.

Rashida's mother, Sabrina, lost her first child when he was only nineteen. Rashida has told me about how much this broke her mother for a while. She had to leave because the grief was overwhelming.

Rashida's niece is named Sabrina, too, after Rashida's mom. But Rashida has always called her niece "Monét" when talking about her. Her middle name. Monét, the first grandchild. Monét, who came out to her grandmother Sabrina before anyone else. Monét, who loved the color purple.

They lost Monét at eighteen.

It's overwhelming to even think about that level of devastation.

I remember the night Hal died was a night New York lost six hundred to seven hundred lives. It was our highest total yet I think. And you talk about it like that, in numbers, in statistics. But people are not numbers.

I didn't ask Rashida what happened to her niece, although I know it's gun violence and it's in Chicago. I don't need to know details. Because the details don't really matter and don't change anything about her grief. She calls me crying later in the week and she tells me she's sick of explaining to people who usually immediately respond to news like that with "What happened?," because mainly I think we don't know what else to say. But I know my sister. If she wants to tell me about it one day, with details, she will. And it will be a day when she's ready and when she wants to talk about it.

I know it's gun violence. I look to see if there is anything written for her niece yet. I don't find anything.

Instead, I read headlines about one hundred people being shot over Father's Day weekend in Chicago. One article mentions two children—a three-year-old and a young teen—both killed by stray bullets.

But it's mainly numbers listed, not names. The numbers people can gaze past while reading the paper, chalking it all up to "gun violence in Chicago." This broad term that is used at best as a way to separate ourselves from the emotional toll and human suffering. At worst it's a term used as a political weapon, usually wielded against the people who've been so traumatized. There's a lot of pain that's been caused by white people. I know I have been confused at how best to be an ally, which is a weird word to say maybe when I really mean friend and sister and fellow human being, because I wasn't sure what I could possibly say that would be the most helpful or have a positive impact. I've been so quiet lately in general.

Monét is not a number. Rashida's brother is not a number. This family did not lose two statistics. Gun violence in Chicago is not a foregone conclusion or something we think of in the abstract as a "societal issue."

Two amazing and beautiful teenagers were taken from a family who loved them so so so much.

Rashida texts me to thank me for the flowers. We laugh a bit because the flowers I sent are beautiful and I'm grateful for the florist who arranged them beautifully with lots of purple flowers and got them delivered quickly during COVID, but she's written my name so large on the ribbon at the bottom of the wreath (which feels strange enough anyway). Only she's written it as "Tecily." Rashida says she'll change it before the small viewing and I say, "If it is something that makes you smile this week, don't you dare change it." The importance of laughter.

After the service, Rashida sends one text.

She's with her uncle now.

I'm so sorry.

JULY 8, 2020

Tommy and Shawn are visiting again. Last night Shawn told us it was the anniversary of his father's passing. We got to speak about him and be with each other and laugh and celebrate him. He says he misses his dad. He chooses to celebrate him on this day. I feel honored to be celebrating him, too.

Tonight, the boys called me outside because I had to see the sky. "Look how pink it is tonight."

And I smiled because I knew it would be pink outside.

It was July 8. Erica's "anniversary."

The day a train went through a tricky intersection and hit my sweet friend headed home to eat her sandwich. An intersection that is no longer so dangerous.

I let the boys know about Erica and how I always think of her during a pink sky. And she gave me one on July 8 during this scary year.

At dinner I toasted Erica and then looked at Shawn and said, "And to your dad."

And he said, "And to my dad."

I sent the beer story to Erica's mom as I toasted with a pink sky behind us. In typical Dee fashion, she wrote me a beautiful note back.

I am crying from your remembrances of Erz, she must be holding you close for writing her story, and I am too. Thank you for writing this piece of her life and sharing it with me. This is golden in my spirit. I love you, will always love you.

Remember you gave her a waffle iron for her birthday one year?

Loving you,
dee

Cheers to dads, friends, pink skies, and waffle irons.

JULY 13, 2020

I sent what I wrote about Rashida to her. She's with her family in Chicago now. I got to FaceTime with her and another one of my favorite people on earth: her mother, Sabrina. Sabrina went through the worst tragedy imaginable when she lost her son, but she still managed to raise some of the most amazing human beings ever. And she always looks amazing.

I spoke to them both, laughing about the show *90 Day Fiancé* because Sabrina and I both are crazy about this silly reality show. We talk about the purse I recently sent Sabrina through a subscription box of gifts. (It's a box from PopSugar that Sabrina calls the "Sugar Pop box," so that's what it will be called from now on.) At one point, Sabrina said it was time for bed. And I knew what she meant. The exhaustion behind that pain. And I felt honored to have gotten that time with her, that she would share it with me. Then I wound up talking to Rashida for a long time. She had her nails done and her hair was looking long and luscious. This always makes me smile like an older sister, seeing this glam version of my sis.

See, out of the five years or so I've known Rashida, I've only ever seen her with her braids and gym shoes, and a manicure to her was what

I called "stubby short nails painted yellow." I'm much more of a drag queen. I like doing my nails and I like big hair and smoky eyes and loud jewelry. Especially if the jewelry is so loud it actually speaks words. Like my new giant earrings that say "Honey" or the necklace I wear daily that says "Lucia" as that's how I sing the song "Maria" from *West Side Story* to Lucy all the time. I think most of my close friends probably have that song memorized now. Doing my part! I like sparkly heels and thigh-high boots and short dresses. I like to play dress-up. I think I've put lashes and wigs on most of my friends at some point or another. But Rashida was still a jeans-and-sneakers girl.

But Rashida started a health and weight loss journey a while ago. We worked out together almost every day the past two or three summers. She looks incredible. And once she started *knowing* that she was looking great, her closet started changing. Suddenly there were dresses, and jumpsuits, and heels. She came to my Christmas show last year and I said, "Well, well, well," as I noticed her long nails. I don't know if you've ever gotten your nails done or worn fake nails, but she started doing that thing we do after a manicure where suddenly you say everything with your hands for emphasis. Gotta show those things off.

Rashida's nails the other day were long and

purple and gold, and they said "Bree" on her fourth finger. Bree is another nickname for her niece. I asked her to send me a picture.

It was good to talk to her. It's been one of the saddest parts of all of this, feeling a disconnect with her. She was in California at my home, and we hadn't talked much. This is a person I talk to every day normally. The number one person. But I think I had an irrational but very real resentment about people outside of New York City not understanding what had happened, and so I didn't want to speak to a lot of people. Then I think she had her own resentment after being out protesting, *leading* protests, in support of Black Lives Matter. I would never, ever be upset with Rashida for any residual anger, though. And even though it may sound odd considering the circumstances, I was so proud, or happy (?)— both words seem wrong—to see my friend being so powerful and maybe even feeling powerful in this moment. I had seen the times people had taken that from her. And there was no chance of that now. I love watching her in action— leading and lifting those around her. It's her life's mission. And she's a force.

JULY 15, 2020

I got a new fairy tale.

Yesterday, Tommy and Shawn and Kevin went on a hike. I'm trying to be more outdoorsy, but I'm not quite a hiker yet. Gardening is sort of as far as I've gotten.

I haven't heard from them for a while, until I see Kevin has texted me. He says, *We got to the top of the mountain and I saw this . . . had to send it to you.*

I look at the picture he sent. It's of a rocky ledge overlooking so many green trees below. And in the middle of one large stone, someone has carved "OWENS." It makes me smile. I thank Kevin. Later, we talk about it, and it's funny because I saw it as a possessive statement. This rock, this view, is Owen's. He read it as "Owen S." I like both.

I immediately decide to send the picture over to the large group text called Owen's Angels that Dr. Henry, Owen's oncologist, started months ago. I think now we are at twelve people: Dr. Henry; myself; Jack; Ed; Laurel; Leda; my dad; Stacia; Syd (the younger actress I promised to mentor someday, but who knows when we will get to meet in person now); Syd's mom, Kerri, the holistic expert; her dad, Ed, a physicist; and another Broadway friend of both Uncle Ed and Dr. Henry whose husband was one of Dr. Henry's patients. Actually, there are two group threads, as my aunt Laurel accidentally started a new one by using her iPad one day. Now we have Owen's Angels 2 as well. That's what happens when a group of twelve texts each other and only two of them are under the age of thirty. I'm surprised we've only had one mess-up!

I send the picture to the group. My dad asks where it is located. I ask Kevin, who tells me, "Kaaterskill Falls." I pass this on to the group.

A moment later I see a text notification from Dad. It says, *Click the map.*

I sent the picture with a little hope inside me that it would lead to a bit more magic. It has happened so often since this spring, these little constellation connections. And I can't wait to see what this one is.

I try to open my dad's map. It doesn't work, of course.

So I go to my map application and type in *Kaaterskill Falls*. And right away I see it.

There are only three names on this map image: Kaaterskill Falls, Spruce Creek, and then there is a little blue marker north of the falls. It says "Laurel House Trail." Laurel—the name of Owen's mom.

Leda says, *Wow! We almost went there for a hike a while back but the trail was closed!*

Then she texts again: *But Owen was there all along.*

Ed chimes in not long after: *And so was Laurel House.*

I think of this as my new fairy tale.

It came after I finally sat to write again, like a sweet reminder of why I've been doing all of this: To find some magic in the midst of all the overwhelming grief and confusion and dangerous chaos. To maybe get a tiny bit closer to knowing how Owen did it. Or maybe to get one step closer to finding some peace for myself, following the lead of my hero. Or at the very least, to let myself see that his story is far from over.

This weekend, I'm finally getting to go up to see Ed, Laurel, Leda, and Leda's boyfriend, Luc. They are about thirty minutes away from us, staying at what we used to call "the country house." I haven't been since I was a kid myself. I remember I got a tick there once, and we spent what felt like hours trying to remove it the right way. My dad and I played in their outdoor pool, my dad doing what I called "butt launchers," where he'd start from under the water beneath me and then he'd spring up, with his hands under my legs, and I'd fly a foot or two out of the water. It was always hilarious to me, probably because it also involved the word *butt*. I held little Leda in my arms and my lap at night, like she was my baby, until one time when she looked up at me and in her funny low husky little five-year-old voice said, "Do you have breasts yet?" The most mortifying question for a twelve-year-old. I spent hours sitting on the floor of the living room, making bird after bird out of Play-Doh because of course that's what Owen wanted to do.

I'm finally going back.

And I'm bringing Jack.

JULY 17, 2020

One thing that's become a weekly tradition since the first week of April, when we were just quarantine babies, is our Saturday Night Virtual Bingo, hosted by the very funny and charming Linda Simpson. She did the show live weekly in New York at Le Poisson Rouge before everything shut down, and Kevin regularly attended. She's always got a different drag queen with her as spokesmodel who shows off the amazing prizes we can win. Last night it was Reina Del Taco. She's one of my faves.

It's been a good way to laugh, especially early on when everything was still so bleak and dismal because we were starting to realize we would be sitting in this bleak and dismal for much longer than we'd expected perhaps. And there were "phases" to coming back to life. Reminds me a bit of a documentary I once saw about coma patients. In movies, I guess (or wherever this sort of false info comes from these days), a person in a coma wakes up one day. Their eyes slowly open, adjust to the light; they look around this unfamiliar room and usually say something like, "What happened? What day is it?"

I'm not saying this is fluff. Or funny in real life. Please know I would only ever make fun of the Hollywood part of any of this. But in this documentary, they followed four patients with brain injuries that led to comas. It was a dark and sometimes hard-to-watch documentary, even for me, but this was during a time my mom was going to school to become a nurse practitioner and her classmate and friend Debbie moved into our guest room for a while. (Megu's room for two years before Debbie. That guest room was really put to use in my house growing up. It might be why I'm so drawn to sharing living spaces with friends now as a grown-up who also highly values alone time.) Debbie was a great laugher, made us the best "gravy" all the time for spaghetti, and watched horrifying medical documentaries. I knew about Ebola long before it became a real fear here and was absolutely terrified during that outbreak, remembering the information I'd gleaned from another documentary I watched with Debbie. I was rehearsing a sketch one week, playing a reporter at a press conference, and I remember talking to Kenan Thompson about it.

"Are you really that scared it could actually get here?"

"I definitely am. I'm terrified. I can't believe that doctor rode the train."

That doctor was one of the incredible human beings who volunteered to fight Ebola where the outbreak was raging in West Africa. But he had returned to New York, and because of tracing methods—that we'd have to actually really learn and use around six years later—we knew he had ridden the subway to Coney Island or something. I remember thinking how irresponsible he was. How could he have been so brazen knowing how easily it was transmitted? Strange to think about now.

Anyway, in the coma documentary I was watching over bowls of spaghetti with Debbie, they were explaining there are different difficult outcomes for head injury patients in comas. Some don't wake up at all. Some do, but they aren't just right back to where they once were. One man was pronounced brain-dead pretty early on, and his family had to make that awful decision. One man in his thirties woke up, but his speech and hearing took a lot of work to return, and it seemed as if his cognitive abilities may have been affected. I remember he had a fiancée, and I found her situation to be so heartbreaking. Because they hadn't gotten to really start life together as a married couple, and it looked as if she would become more of a caretaker to her partner rather than a wife. There was a teen girl who came out of her coma strong and was able to speak pretty quickly. During her training, however, her mom looked on worried as she heard all the bad words flying out of her daughter's mouth as she screamed at the nurses. The nurses explained this was totally normal and a part of the healing, because of whichever part of her brain was affected and now starting to heal with hard work. Then there was a very sad case of a boy who'd been attacked while on a trip overseas. It was clear later on that although he had "woken up," the doctors didn't believe he'd ever regain real consciousness. He would just be stuck in a wheelchair, mouth agape, unable to do anything on his own, for the rest of his "life." But his family couldn't let him go. That's one of those situations that somehow are even crueler because so many have become politicized. How can a family even begin to think about the right thing to do without their tragedy becoming a spectacle? How much more weight can you add to that decision? It's so unfair. My mom, the semiretired nurse practitioner, being the sometimes clinically cold but efficient mother that she is, has always made sure to outline all of her end-of-life wants. I think my brother and I get a text or email once or twice a year, explaining her will and making sure we both have the copies and understand everything (as if that's reading material I can't wait to dive right into, Mom); explaining how she wants her remains to be either donated to science or cremated and used as a reef ball to help rebuild a coral reef; and, most important to my mom, and the point she pushes the most, explaining how she does not want to be resuscitated. She even called me once explaining she was thinking of giving power of attorney to her best friend instead of my brother or me, because she wasn't sure we would be able to do it, and her best friend had promised her. I'm not sure where that stands today, but I certainly haven't forgotten her rules. I often have to remind her I'm not a medical professional and it's not quite as easy for me to compartmentalize my thinking in that situation. After one too many emails, I sometimes just have to say, "Can we stop talking about you dying, Mom?" Then she gets it. She'll just have to trust I have that info stored in the back of my mind someplace where I don't have to think about it.

Well, that was a long walk. Back to my point about the comas: It seems we all had an idea when the pandemic started that we would be the Hollywood version and we'd wake up and say, "What day is it?" And someone would say, "Twenty twenty-one. COVID is over. You're safe now." And all would go back to normal. But in fact we've had to talk about "reopening" American society. And it's done in phases. We will have to come back to life in phases, and I'm sure we will all need varying degrees of physical therapy to heal, to feel like we know how to exist in our environments and move around, and it will take work. There will be some damage that's irreversible: physically, mentally, societally. There will be some miracles. There will be devastating heartbreaks. What started as a scary moment has become something that does not feel like it even belongs to our generations anymore. The story will be told by historians however many years in the future, and they will be the ones with the answers we don't seem likely to get, and they'll have the questions we weren't even aware enough yet to ask. They'll have a name for this period of time, however many years it lasts. So it's not quite ours anymore, but we are still here and we are the ones who will live through it. It feels like we are the doctors using leeches. Or the policemen saving evidence at the many crime scenes in Sacramento in the 1970s and '80s, knowing the science wasn't there yet but might be someday, laying the groundwork for an older man to be arrested in 2018 for being the elusive East Area Rapist and Original Night Stalker (EARONS) after forensics linked his DNA to family members who had voluntarily submitted their own DNA to these genetic ancestry websites that would become popular in the 2010s. (I'm a bit of a true-crime nut. Rashida's nickname for me is even "DCI Strong.")

Okay, but back to bingo. Kevin has bought cards for us every weekend except for the Fourth of July holiday weekend because they were off that week. Looking at a calendar now, we must have played around fifteen weekends so far during quarantine. Us and the other drag bingo regulars, like Chain-Smoking Patty, and ninety-year-old dancing queen Winnie, and Viv, who is quarantined with her children in New York over the Italian restaurant they own, and the shirtless quartet of men with mustaches in San Francisco. It's become our "neighborhood" in a way. We have a community. Jack has played twice. We played at the dinner table with his family once—they have a house not too far away in the Berkshires and everybody there had been isolating—and they loved it so much his sister decided to book Linda for her virtual baby shower. It's nice to be able to share that kind of joy and laughter anytime, but especially right now.

JULY 18, 2020

Jack and I drove up to the country house to see Ed and Laurel and Leda and celebrate Leda's birthday. Enough time had passed with everyone being isolated out of the city that they were okay with visitors. It's only the second time I've seen Leda since the service, and I think the first time I've seen my uncle Ed and Laurel—although we speak on our Owen's Angels group text.

On the drive up, I tell Jack it's been so long since I was here. I know the house was totally redone, so I won't recognize it. As we turn onto the driveway, I start to cry a little. I don't want to really examine why I'm crying at this moment, but I want to let myself cry because I don't want to cry in front of them. I still have my little promise with Owen. And I want Leda to have a nice birthday dinner.

We get there and I immediately hug Leda, who has come out to greet us after I called worried by the lack of cars in the driveway that somehow we were at the wrong house. We aren't. I hug my beautiful little sun-goddess cousin in her pool getup. She's been surprised by two Peruvian friends for the birthday weekend, Lia and Fernando. Fernando is a good friend from her sports management program at Columbia.

It's also where she met her German boyfriend, Luc, who is also at the country house with her. We've been assured everyone has been properly quarantining before the dinner. In fact, it seems to be Jack and me who worry them the most, as we are seated at a smaller table off of the bigger table outside, further distanced from the group. But it makes me feel safer somehow that I'm seen as the biggest COVID threat, knowing what a hermit I've been. Give me the kids' table any day!

Quite a chic little group, Leda and her friends. Attractive and tan multilingual twenty-somethings drinking rosé and seltzers. I wonder how they see Jack and me. Well, not so much Jack. He's an athlete and he's closer to their age. I'm the thirty-six-year-old cousin who's never worn a bikini in her life who rolled up with rainbow floats for the pool. I also am constantly running away from what Leda has explained to me are "cicada-killing wasps," which seem to love her pool. I am terrified of all bugs and always have to explain, "It's not rational, I know they won't hurt me, but I have to run so please just ignore me because that's really the only solution."

I introduce Jack to Laurel and Ed as well. I can't stop smiling, I'm so happy to see them. In the sunshine. Ed says it's Saturday, which is the day our dear friend Dr. Henry does his weekly call. We decide to all do the call together by the pool. Dr. Henry is delighted to hear that I'm there with them. And then he sounds shocked and almost happier than I am that Jack is there. I realize I haven't quite filled in Dr. Henry on the situation that my broken heart isn't really broken anymore. Dr. Henry does as he usually does, and he tells us more news updates and complains about Trump, and we all say goodbye. I'm so thankful for Dr. Henry again, and for expanding the group text and the family, therefore, in a way. Because it also expands Owen's story.

Jack and I change into our suits in Owen's room. I am hesitant going in, but upon entering, it doesn't feel as if I'm intruding on a sacred space. It doesn't seem like it's been totally redone or totally left alone since Owen passed. It was his room in the country house, and he's a pretty neat person, and so I don't think he'd have much of thirty-year-old Owen's things strewn about. Not like in his home in New York. It's how I decide to think of it anyway. It's a bright and friendly room. I point to a big block of carved wood on the wall. It says "Owen Strong" in kind of childlike writing, and I assume he painted that little sign at some point. I smile at it.

We eat an early dinner because Laurel doesn't want us to stay too late and have to drive in the dark. I'm probably even more anxious about driving at night around here. All the deer. We have corn with spiced butter and chicken and coleslaw, and it's all delicious of course. Ed tells me the water jug we are using once belonged to my grandfather Cecil. He would use it to make his old-fashioneds. Leda walks away with Lia for a while. I wonder how she's doing. I start to feel anxious and I try to get the gears in motion to leave. I explain we have bingo at eight. I tell them all about it.

I give Leda a dumb little sheet of paper I've printed out of the jewelry I sent to her house on Martha's Vineyard, worried it wouldn't get to me in time. I wasn't sure what to get her this year. I didn't want to try to do something huge and fabulous because that doesn't feel really appropriate. And I didn't want to go the generic route and get her some basketball thing. (Every Christmas for years, I've gotten gifts related to wine or dogs or both. Like a shirt that says, "I only want to rescue dogs and drink wine." I haven't even really been drinking wine for seven years, because I like it too much and I'm always on a mini diet for TV, so I drink vodka or tequila and a lot of soda water. But I'm drinking lots of wine these days.) So I decided to look on my favorite jewelry website. They have a store in Brooklyn, not that I've ever gone. But I love to wear big loud jewelry. Everyone that day is asking about my beaded rainbow chain leading to the gold "Lucia" written around my neck. I explain I had it made because Lucia is what I call Lucy when I'm serenading her with my version of the song "Maria" from *West Side Story*. Everybody just kind of nods as if that makes perfect sense.

I know there is a bit of a little-sister element in my relationship with Leda. She has bought herself dresses I've worn. I know she looks up to me as much as I feel a similarly strong pride in watching over her as her older cousin. And so in that spirit, I bought her some jewelry I think is fun. Some sparkly dangly watermelon-slice earrings. A gold necklace with a hanging rainbow-jeweled "L" pendant. And lastly, a pair of colorful bird earrings. I love the birds.

I give her just that paper because I went back and forth about a card. I realize how emotionally unprepared I was for this trip. I don't want to write something short and generic that just feels unimportant or even sort of dismissive. On the other hand, if I wrote her an actual letter, it would be as long as one of these essays, and I don't want to drop a heavy book into her lap on this nice summer day to celebrate her birthday.

I go up and change again in Owen's room. I know I have to go. We've got to go while everyone is still smiling. That's the only way I know how to explain it. It's Leda's birthday, and it's summer, and I want to leave them that way. I kiss my hand and touch the sign. Goodbye, Owen.

I hug Leda again and kiss her head. I'm happy leaving her in the hands of her wonderful friends. I hug Laurel, and I'm glad she's got Leda and Leda's friends to sort of look after. She also has an amazing garden. She offers to give me some planters but I decline eventually because I just bought four more and I can't go full hoarder in this Airbnb.

It's hardest to say goodbye to Ed. It feels like maybe he doesn't want us to go? I don't know. He comes out and Jack shows him the "Stang." That's how Jack refers to his pride and joy, his 2008 black Mustang GT (and you better believe I had to text Jack to get those details right). I don't know if Ed likes cars this much, but he's doing a great job of feigning interest otherwise. It's sweet. I'm so lucky he's my uncle. This gentle gentle man seeing me out and being so welcoming to Jack, telling him he hopes to see him again. I hug Ed again and immediately I start to cry. Jack puts his hand on my leg. I can't explain to him either why I needed to go when I did. I just knew staying meant saying words that were too heavy for me and all of us. The weight of grief in losing a person like Owen. Because every day he isn't there, it feels like a loss still. It will never be a vacant space. It will always be an active absence.

I say I hope Leda is okay. I think these markers are always a little superficial, but it's not just her first birthday without Owen. It's the first summer. I think about going back to the country house for me. Even though the house is different, that has just marked my first time revisiting a space connected to Owen now that he's gone. Jack says they all seem a little quiet. I laugh and I say, "Owen was loud. He was the loud one." And I feel again that's why I had to leave. I didn't want to cry in front of them, and I needed to cry. I am so happy we got to smile together and hug and eat good food and enjoy the sunshine. I'm glad they met Jack. I tell Jack I think it matters to them to see me happy. "Meeting you not only lets them know I'm happier but is a way to bring them an energy of life moving forward in nice ways too."

I don't want to ever be stuck in that very sad trap of thinking your happiness lives in your memories now. I want to know that my happiness and the love for Owen we all had and got to experience moves forward with us as well. I slip into the role I think Owen would like when I'm there: Making them smile. Taking care of Leda. Making sure Leda never ever feels like she's not enough just by not being Owen.

We are almost home when I tell Jack that it still feels so special and so lucky that I got to tell my cousins as often as I did how much I loved them. That I got to hear it back. That we weren't afraid to say it to each other, especially after a GBM diagnosis. I had the most wonderful relationship with my two amazing cousins, and it is the most precious gift ever to know I got the opportunity to hug them both often and to send sappy texts letting them know how much I loved them. And I got to hear it back just as often. I'm lucky.

But it's hard. It's still so sad. I'm still crying hard heavy tears today as I write this.

We get home right around eight. Kevin has bingo all set up. I take a couple minutes to blow my nose and hug and kiss Lucy. As the second game starts, I take Lucy outside for the bathroom and to get some air.

"You're two away, though," says Kevin.

"It's fine," I say. "I never win bingo. Will you just watch my card?"

I'm outside with Lucy.

"You're one away," he hollers.

"I'm not going to win," I holler back. "You know I never do."

"You just got bingo!"

I go back inside and look to see that I have indeed gotten a bingo. I'm the only one. Linda pulls up our Zoom screen. I say, "Hi." I'm so nervous because I've never won. The prize is what she calls "Crazy Cow." I assume it's a stuffed animal and it is: a cow with his arms and legs outstretched like he wants a full-body hug or has fallen on his back and needs help up. He's smiling. The best part is the giant tuft of white hair on his head. Like Doc in *Back to the Future*.

Linda does her fun twist where she offers me the cow or whatever is in the mystery bag. Usually people take the mystery bag just to see. I say I want to stick with the cow because I've never won bingo and that Crazy Cow is how I won, and I will honor the cow!

I text Leda that night. I tell her again how much I love her and loved seeing her.

I also tell her I won bingo for the first time.

I hope she sees, like I do, that it doesn't feel like a coincidence, but rather a reminder.

See Cec. You ARE lucky.

AUGUST 16, 2020

I haven't been able to listen to his music since April.

It's odd because before I was able to really talk about Owen, I found the best way to share him was sending people his music. Now that I can talk and write about him, I can't seem to listen to the music.

Owen was in a band called the Evening Fools. I think I first heard about them while staying in an Airbnb in Maitland, Florida, for my stepsister's wedding. I got my brother and myself an Airbnb with a pool. The house was funny and kitschy. I remember a lot of those "silly" signs people put up on their walls. Ones that say things like: "Rules for this pool: the bar is always open." "Don't do anything that starts with 'Hey, y'all, watch this.'" "Clothing is optional, but not recommended (especially for women)." "We don't skinny dip, we chunky dunk." "We don't swim in your toilet so please don't pee in our pool." That kind of thing. Our first Airbnb in the Hudson Valley had a lot of those. "Just breathe and accept the crazy." The one in my room said, "Always kiss me good night."

We were in Maitland for the wedding. One afternoon, my dad and Owen came over for happy-hour drinks at the "always open bar" out back by the pool. We were sitting around chatting and my dad started asking Owen about his music.

My dad is a big music lover as well. He played guitar in high school, doing a lot of Donovan covers. I remember seeing an old high school yearbook of his, and most of the kids who had signed his book said something about "watching Billy rocking out on his guitar."

My dad revisited music not long before he and my mom split up. I add that detail because I think a man starting a country rock cover band in his forties is just such a textbook warning sign that a divorce is probably imminent. His band was called the Clinton Home Band and consisted of my dad and a group of local friends. Most lived on Clinton Avenue (my street) or Home Avenue, which were right next to each other. I used to play Capture the Flag and Cops and Robbers with the kids on Home Avenue because they seemed to always be out. Clinton was less active, except for when my childhood friend's dad, the man I knew as a "Vietnam vet," who lived down the street, would scream throughout his house. Mrs. Clark, who lived across the street from us, would be outside smoking a cigarette and say, "This is why you don't do drugs, kids." So Home Avenue was much more friendly to kids' games in the summer.

The rest of the band was a group of adults I

knew in different ways but now watched playing in my dad's band at block parties. There was my mom's really close friend Ronda, whom she met at the Episcopal church we all attended until I decided it was not for me around seventh grade. (I tried Unitarianism for a second, but my friend Melissa asked me to stop going to her youth group because she thought a boy she liked was starting to like me. So that ended my being a Unitarian youth.)

Then there was Mr. Jacobson. I can't call him by his first name, although he has one, because he was my music teacher for all of elementary school. A patient and gentle man, who at his most frustrated by a rowdy class would start patting his head and snapping his fingers to get us to repeat the sequence of taps and snaps and pats he had just done. He made sure we sang Hanukkah songs, Kwanzaa songs, and Spanish-language songs at the Holiday Sing. Very Oak Park. I still know how to say good night in nine different languages because of him. And he always let me have an easy instrument solo, usually a recorder or Orff instrument, because I of course always wanted a solo. I had to make a pink yarn lanyard for my recorder during our performance of "Go My Son," which we were told was a Native American song (but who knows). I had to drop my recorder because the song also involved sign language. He directed the sixth graders every year singing "One Tin Soldier" during our Memorial Day program. He had us all sing "This Used to Be My Playground" when they tore down our school playground to build a more modern and safer one. Our playground before then was called "the forts" because it consisted of a number of tall wooden structures meant for kids to climb up and down. But these structures were also laid out so they were separated by just the right amount of space to make kids decide, "I should jump that," which of course meant that kids were always getting hurt and breaking bones.

Then I am pretty sure my friend Joan's dad was in the band. He was another quiet, sweet man, whose son became a full-time real-life musician, according to Facebook, I think.

And last, on lead guitar (sorry, Dad) was Mike Casey. He was a quiet cowboy-looking man who ran a music shop, Guitar Fun, where he'd also provide lessons. He was in a lot of local bands, always playing at a bar called FitzGerald's. My dad threw my eighth birthday party there, because a children's silly country band named Riders in the Sky was playing, and I sobbed in my dad's arms when they tried to sing to me. (For some reason, I was horribly uncomfortable whenever being serenaded. One of the most popular restaurants in my town growing up, and one my parents especially loved, was a Mexican place called La Majada that featured a nightly mariachi band going table to table to serenade diners. I cringe when I think back on how awkward it must have been singing to our table as child Cecily slid down underneath and sobbed until they left. Luckily, as an adult, I seem to have gotten past whatever that was.)

Mike Casey never quite looked like he belonged in Oak Park. He didn't even really look like he belonged in the Midwest. I thought of him more as a Western guy, like someone who might live in Arizona or New Mexico or whatever my brain assumed was "Western" back then. My friend Liz had a closer relationship with him throughout her life, as her whole family was involved in the local music scene. Liz and her sister Laura had some of the best voices I've ever heard. There is a recording of Liz singing "Leaving on a Jet Plane" that was particularly poignant after we lost her. And I'll never forget Laura the night of Liz's service, getting up to sing "Rhiannon" at a karaoke bar pretty much empty except for this group of sad people drinking together after a long, sad funeral with no casket. Laura closed her eyes and held her head up and hit every note with the pain of seven years of watching her closest friend and little sister battle an impossible addiction leading to the night Liz fell over in her chair in front of her computer, leaving her parents to find her in the morning.

Mike Casey actually passed away a couple of

years ago. I don't quite know when or how. He was always sort of a folklore figure to me, and not someone too close, so I knew of his passing, but it didn't affect me the same way. I do remember thinking that for such a quiet person, it was a big loud loss to the local music community. He played with all of them, in so many shows, head down, always there.

When my dad moved out of the house, he found an apartment pretty quickly at a new complex that had been recently built in Oak Park: the Prairie Home Apartments. The Clinton Home Band played a show there not long after, celebrating the new complex. I remember I was sitting on the metal handrail above the concrete steps leading to the courtyard, with my friend Joan, listening to my dad taking the lead vocals and singing about taking a load off Fanny, or everybody jumping for joy when Quinn the Eskimo gets here, or taking a little trip in 1814 with Colonel Jackson down the mighty Mississip'. Then of course he'd sing the song he wrote in college called "Famous Last Words." (It was a cheeky song, in that the verse was about someone who died heroically and it would lead into the chorus with something like "and right before the plane hit the ground he said, 'Oh f—' —amous last words, echo through history.") The Clinton Home Band was playing to a pretty crowded group at dusk, and I was swinging my legs on the rail above the steps. At some point, I swung too hard and I fell forward, fast, my face smashing into the concrete. I remember the gritty, almost sandy feeling of pain across my face. In fact, I used to have nightmares where I would dive off a diving board but miss the pool, and I'd feel that sandy hard feeling on my face again.

I don't know how long the Clinton Home Band lasted, but not too much longer. I think my dad played on his fiftieth birthday at FitzGerald's. We had a rough couple of years in high school. I was eighteen then, in my senior year at the academy. I don't know if my memory has the timing exactly right, but I am pretty sure that my dad called to talk to me about coming to his party. He said how much it would mean to him for me to be there, and he was sorry for all the times he had hurt me or not been the best dad he could've been. I don't know if I would have gone if not for that talk. I love my dad, my first best friend, but we've had a lot of rocky ups and downs, which makes our relationship today all the more special to me.

So, it's 2016 in Maitland, Florida, and I'm at this quirky house with a pool with funny signs, and my dad and Owen are hanging out on chairs with me, and my dad says, "Hey, can we hear some of your songs?"

Owen lights up. I didn't know he was making music! He says he's just kind of playing around with a couple of friends. We play his music on the speaker system.

"Is that *you* singing?" I ask.

He smiles shyly and says, "Yeah."

Owen is so good.

I knew various parts of Owen's life. I knew he was in that a cappella group in college, but I didn't know of this band. Owen's band is the Evening Fools. I don't hear much more about them for a while. Then, on February 15, 2019, he sends me a text.

Owen: Hey cuz! Check out the new jam on Spotify.

I already love the illustration accompanying the song. It's a man in a Panama hat and jeans looking like he's comfortably snoozing while a giant hand is cradling him. A red bird is flying overhead and there is a lighthouse in the distance. The song is called "Do as It May."

I listen. I listen again.

Cecily: Ow, it's so good! I'm legit crying! You sound great! When did you do this one??? And how many of you are making the songs? It's really great.

I text again. I'm excited.

Cecily: I'm sharing with some friends hope you don't mind!

Owen: Thank you so much cec! That truly makes me so happy to hear!

This song becomes a pretty big song in our lives.

Owen dances with his girlfriend, Stacia, at his thirtieth birthday bash while a band plays his song for him. A video from the party was played at his service. He and Stacia are smiling wide and huge, swaying with their arms around each other, and Owen and the crowd are singing along.

The lyrics are printed on the first page of the program Leda made for his service.

Before I am able to talk about Owen, after he's gone, I share his music as a way to share this person I don't know how to grieve yet. I remember two responses that meant so much.

One of my stage managers at work is named Gena, and she and I have been close since the beginning. She's a little rock-and-roller chick who used to work at MTV during the nineties, and we tease her about this constantly. She lets us. She loves us.

Gena has a son, G., whom I absolutely adore. I met him first when he was around nine years old. Sometimes Gena worries about him, and I like to talk with her and remind her life is bigger than high school and G. is so magical and kind and courageous and talented. He rocks on his guitar. He gets leads in musicals. He dons a scary mask and stands right up front as his performing arts school dances to "Thriller" on Halloween.

Gena texts me: *Played Owens music for G. Didn't tell him anything about him. He said, "Angel music."*

My friend Jenn is a wonderful person with the biggest heart and made us Christmas flower headpieces when she came to *SNL*. I send her Owen's music. She is on the set of her show in New Orleans. She texts me: *Cecily, I was just listening to the other Owen song. And my co-worker Kevin came into my trailer because he was walking by and liked how it sounded and we sat together and listened.*

There is something I love about people being stopped in their tracks by his music.

Jenn says "the other Owen song" because Owen finished a song right before going back into the hospital for what nobody knew would be the last time. Uncle Ed told me about it that first night I saw them in the now quiet apartment after Owen flew away.

Ed told me Owen was adamant about finishing this song. It's an older one that they left for a while, but he wanted to go back to it. Ed said that at first Owen and his bandmates were only going to play songs using the instruments they could play. But Ed convinced Owen to be open to adding studio musicians. And so Owen added strings. He didn't play any string instrument, but he arranged them for this song.

Ed gave me his headphones and I sat down at the table and listened to one of the most beautiful songs I've ever heard. It's called "Stay the Night." Owen sounds beautiful. He sounds ethereal. I am so glad Owen somehow knew he had to finish this song when he did. I'm so glad I get to listen to it and to him.

And then in April, at the first Airbnb, I stand outside and start to listen to the song. I have to stop it.

I can't do it.

It's too hard right now.

And I haven't tried again since. Not yet.

AUGUST 17, 2020

On his thirtieth birthday, I am already feeling guilty that I cannot be there because I have a show. I come up with a great idea for a present. At this point, Owen has been home a lot because of treatments, and I think his friends have gotten him every book and board game and boxed set of every show. I want to get something different. I have an idea. I reach out to my agent to help. It seems positive. I wait and wait, but the present doesn't arrive and his birthday passes.

I text him: *Happiest of birthdays! I'm so sorry I'm missing tonight. Was working on getting Shaggy to record a message for you and fell through last minute so now I'm empty handed like an asshole! I hope tonight is the best ever and I can't wait to hear about it tomorrow! Lots and lots of love! Welcome to your 30's!!!*

Owen: *Hey cuz! Thank you so much for even trying to pull that off! You're the best! Wish you could come too, so excited to see you tomorrow!*

We're planning on hanging out. Then he remembers he's going to his girlfriend's family house the next day for "the *Thrones* premiere."

Me: *I miss you! Let's do din soon!*

Three days later I get a video:

"Hey, Owen, what's up, this is Shaggy."

He goes on and wishes Owen a happy birthday. It's amazing. Shaggy came through!

I text Owen: *Welp. The surprise is ruined but I hope it's still cool :) Shout out to karaoke 2012 when I was auditioning.*

Owen: *WHAAAAT??!!! Holy shit this is so friggin amazing! Thank you so much cuz! I can't believe you pulled this off. You are the absolute best! Oh man. Thank you thank you! I love you.*

Me: *I thought "what do you get the guy who has literally read and watched everything over the past year :)"*

Then: *And I wanted you to know how much your friendship (which I can say because family doesn't always imply friendship) has meant to me all these years. The support and love has never gone unnoticed and I'm a better person because of your family but especially you and Leda. And this past year, I watched a real life superhero. And that's all I'll say about that.*

AUGUST 18, 2020

They talk about "the big one" when they talk about California earthquakes. There's a fault line under the state, and if it rips, California will be torn apart and cast into the ocean. But I've always been more afraid of the fires. They've become so big and so deadly and so frequent. They can swallow up a thousand people in two days. At points, it seems they are partly contained, but all it takes is a shift in the weather, and the fire rages even stronger and new blazes are set and the firefighters have to find new strategies, more water in a state that was almost out of water not long ago.

AUGUST 21, 2020

It's late August now and I'm feeling myself start to slowly get sad.

I've always been sad this time of year. I remember not quite having the vocabulary as a kid to describe how I could smell the end of summer in the air and it would make me want to cry. It's like I've been on the run, wild, and that's what summer is. Possibilities. And now I'm slowing down, heading into fall, work, responsibility, cold weather, and darker days, and I have to look side to side to start taking inventory of what I've gained and what I've lost somehow along the way.

I am holding on to the summer as much as I can. To the feeling I've gotten to have, lying in the sunshine with Lucy. Laughing at Jack's pool at his family's beautiful home in the Berkshires; Jack has moved up there pretty much permanently now, so I get to see him often. Laughing hard with Kevin and Tommy and Shawn. Winning bingo! Making cucumber soup once a week, using herbs I grew myself. Getting to hold Jack's hand as much as I have. Wearing summer dresses and drinking really good wine. And I've felt safe.

Yesterday was the last night of the Democratic National Convention. I've always been a bit of a political wonk and it's mainly because of my dad. He worked for a PR firm in Chicago most of my life growing up, and they wound up working a lot with the Democratic Party in Chicago. Every election, I've turned to my dad, thinking he'll have answers and sometimes hoping he'll fix what's happening.

So, naturally, we are all texting about the DNC on the Owen's Angels thread.

It's a bizarre convention. It's all virtual. There isn't a crowd to address, just sometimes a wall of screens. Everyone is in masks. Our new normal. I don't notice really anymore. That was fast.

I'm feeling as optimistic as possible about Joe Biden. Because whether or not I feel like he has all the plans and answers to "fix" everything, which I actually don't believe is a realistic expectation anyway and is in fact disingenuous, I believe that Joe Biden cares about people. Actively. And it's his purpose. And it's his purpose because of grief and loss.

It's strange and maybe sad to think about having an election where we are looking for someone else who has been hurt because we need to acknowledge our own losses. It's not about a personality or money or taxes or not liking Donald Trump. Americans have just gone through an insane amount of loss over a short period of time. We are at 170,000 and counting deaths from COVID. And it's not frustrating anymore. It's not frustrating that these people won't wear masks. It's not frustrating that people held parties trying to get COVID. It's *beyond* frustrating. It's exhausting and it's devastating and everyone is mourning. And we can't truly express our sympathies to each other because we are still grieving ourselves.

One of my favorite drag queens, Chi Chi DeVayne, passed away yesterday. At thirty-four. Of kidney failure. And I think losing this young, amazingly special and kind person is so sad on its own. I don't know where to put that loss. What pile does that go in as I am internally trying to organize this giant messy sadness inside me? I wonder how to grieve. I wonder if the bits of sad I feel every day can cover all of it. I don't want to start feeling too tired to be sad, to cry. Because I don't want to ever ever let myself start thinking of those numbers not as people. With loved ones. Whole families wiped out.

So I like Joe Biden because he carries his grief with him. Sometimes at your lowest, you can only feel better by giving yourself a purpose. Throwing yourself into work you'd never imagined being part of your life, but here you are. And it's interesting to see that I think that's what is bonding people over Joe Biden. He lives with grief honestly, which I think makes us feel like he will acknowledge and care about ours. Just like that chef José Andrés said this summer:

compassion is the only way to beat the pandemic. Here is our chance. I really hope we take it.

There was a moment last night at the strange but powerful virtual DNC that I keep thinking about. It's a video of his children and grandchildren talking about Joe. And it's the normal kind of political video where we see so-and-so is a family man so he will care about yours, etc. But then, at the end, there's a sound clip and a quote. It's Beau Biden saying, "I can't be there to support my dad this fall, so I'm asking you to be there."

Beau Biden passed away from GBM. Young. Accomplished. Brave. Smart. And someone says something about Beau not being here but still guiding his father every day. And my dad texts me, *Reminds me of Ed and Owen.*

And he's right. It does. It's simple. But it makes me feel hopeful for Uncle Ed. That there is a way to hold that gigantic grief and not have to deal with it by trying to forget someone ever existed because it's too hard to know they aren't here anymore.

But here's Beau Biden, his voice captured sometime, someplace, before here and now, and he's with all of us at the same virtual DNC. His story isn't over either.

GBM is cruel. Cancer is so fucking cruel. It's unreal.

So I'm happy about Joe Biden. And I'm glad people seem to be moving away from the kind of grief that makes you want others to hurt, too. Moving to the grief where your only solace is helping others.

There's just too much cruelty. So much cruelty that it feels like it even stopped the Earth from turning.

And so I think I'm afraid of what happens when the weather changes and the sun doesn't shine anymore. I'm afraid to take that inventory.

I really hope Joe Biden wins in November.

I really miss you, Owen, and I wish you were here in this time and space.

Though, is he? What about the lightbulb?

I've always sort of felt like I had a weird "thing" with electricity, especially when I moved into my apartment in New York in 2012. I remember a day my first year or so in New York. I was feeling particularly low and lonely, and when I got home, I discovered all my lightbulbs had burned out. In the kitchen, entry, and living room. I had to replace every lightbulb. And my friends used to joke about my "ghost in the printer" because I had a printer that seemed to have a mind of its own; even though it had been powered off for hours, it would just start printing (just a blank sheet of paper) or turning itself on. This was especially jarring in the middle of the night when you know you shouldn't be hearing the sounds of an office in your dark, empty apartment. I went to a medium once and when I asked her if my apartment was haunted, she said it was me. Apparently I had boundary issues: with people in this life and people on the other side.

The week I got back to New York after Owen passed, I had a couple of weird electricity moments. And they were both in my bathroom. The day before I was going over to the apartment to see Leda, Ed, and Laurel, I was sitting on the toilet, shock and grief making me move so slowly even just to pee. I was sitting on the toilet in a daze and something caught my eye. I have an electronic scale on the floor, and it turns itself off unless you turn it on. That night, for about five seconds or so, the scale started flashing random numbers like a calculator breaking or something. It stopped after I'd had long enough to realize what had happened. I didn't think too much of it but still mentioned it to Leda. Just in case.

The next day, right before dinner, I was in my bathroom again getting ready to leave and one of the three lightbulbs over my sink started to flicker. And I wasn't sure if it was my eyes or the light flickering. So I looked at it for a bit, trying to adjust my eyes. And then it made a popping sound and the light flashed and went out completely. Not totally an explosion, in that it didn't shatter, but it certainly was a bit of a show. It made me smile a little, because I had been unsure about the flashing numbers on the scale and the flickering light, so this was like being hit over the head, like, *Here! Is this obvious enough for you?!?!* And in that moment I think I laughed a little and then thought, *Okay, I get it, and bathrooms are funny and it's hard to find things funny right now but can the bathroom* not *be our place?*

So I will keep my eyes open in case I see him elsewhere, in the birdsong or the daffodils or exploding bathroom lightbulbs.

AUGUST 29, 2020

We are watching TV, the three of us: Kevin, Jack, and I. It's an episode of *Singletown*, which is a British dating show. We are laughing about the fashion choices and all the other stupid mindless details that make reality TV shows easy and silly and never too heavy. We are laughing and Jack grabs my wrist to look at his phone. I see what it says and quickly turn away.

"No," I say. "Not now. Not now."

We try to keep watching but I'm too sad now.

"What happened?" Kevin asks.

I can see Jack overly mouthing: "Chadwick. Boseman. Died. Cancer."

Okay, fine, now we have to look. It's out there and too sad to even want to read or acknowledge it's true. But I have to. It says he'd been battling colon cancer for four years. Four years. Everyone starts doing math, counting backward, realizing all the things he did WHILE BEING TREATED FOR COLON CANCER. He filmed the greatest action movie of all time, and it was even more of a SUPERhero of a movie because it was the first to feature mainly all Black actors. It made an unbelievable amount of money and actually changed the world, in a Hollywood sense but also in that more important sense of children seeing a supercool hero movie where the heroes look like them. All of them!

I know an amazing woman in Chicago who is part of creating Wakandacon, which is tough for me to explain because I'VE NEVER BEEN TO A CONVENTION. So I only know the basic idea: there are speakers and workshops on all sorts of topics and everybody can dress up as superheroes. My friend Marketta gets to showcase her artwork and dance and music classes. Rashida of course does some kind of press or hosting and general hype-man shit. I know she does plenty of logistical things as well to help, but this is where she *shines*. Rashida takes videos of people to share on social media for the event. Rashida *saves* a video of a specific boy. She's flirting with him and giggling behind the camera. He says, "Hey, Auntie." She shrieks.

"Rashida!" I say. "He looks sixteen!"

"No, he works at a school with my friend."

Later I'm eating dinner with her and Marketta and I can't let Marketta miss out on teasing Rashida about this young hunk. Marketta sees the picture and screams out, "He's sixteen!" We do some very light detective work and see he does work at a school, so we eventually give in a little and say we will believe he's a TA or something and he's nineteen. Rashida tells us they went on a terrible date together.

"What?!?" we scream.

He took her to an Illinois-based wine restaurant chain. In the suburbs.

"WHAT?!?"

She's a Chicago girl through and through. South Side Chicago. And he took her to the suburbs? Okay. He ordered the wine for them, very proud of his own chivalry; when it got to the table, she saw it was called "Romance Red." I make barfing sounds.

"And I think he made a toast to new beginnings or something," Rashida said. "But I was already out."

We laughed about it all night.

Rashida had to go in for a pretty big surgery in the last couple of years. She's okay, thank God, and the surgery seems to have really improved her health and life, but big surgeries are traumatic on your body. She has not had an easy go bouncing back, but she's working really fucking hard. She always works really fucking hard.

At that surgery, so many people texted me to ask whether I had spoken to her and whether she was okay. She was out of surgery but needed to stay a couple of days. I talk to her on the day she's supposed to be sent home, held together by staples basically and on a crazy amount of pain pills. I'm walking to work as Rashida tells me she's going to just order a Lyft. "A Lyft? What??? No! You cannot get in a Lyft right now while you are high as hell and with a giant stomach wound! Call a friend!"

I'm screaming on Broadway and Fifty-Seventh. But so is everybody. She's so used to helping others. She doesn't realize this means there are lines of people who would love to return the favor to her someday. She promises to text her cousin. At the end of our call, she says her cousin said she can get her. DUH.

While she was in the hospital some people texted me the room number, suggesting I could send flowers. I wasn't able to be there because of work. So I really don't like people suggesting "gifts" to me, as if I'm not her sister. Her older sister who's already got a plan. When she gets to finally leave the hospital to start her recovery at home, her brother says there's a gift for her. We are on the phone. She says, "Sis, you get me alcohol?" (Which is still so funny to me, like I sent her a jug of whiskey or something.)

"Well, maybe you should open it," I say.

It takes a second of what I can hear is Rashida opening the box, turning the bottle around, saying, "Huh?" And then lightly reading out loud, "Romance Red . . . ROMANCE RED OH MY GOD."

So, here we are after a smile: *Black Panther* changed lives. And Chadwick Boseman was the STAR. The hero to save the world. Black Panther. I think of Leda immediately. All these articles are beautiful and they all mention how his fight wasn't public. His illness was kept private. I wouldn't dare speculate on this here because there are so many reasons to talk or not talk.

Leda texts me the next morning: *Hi! I miss you How are you?? I also have to tell you about an experience last night that sounds unbelievable but that I know you'll believe.*

I smile. I was just thinking of texting her. Me: *Oh yes please tell me! And I was going to text you anyway. Because of the sad coincidence that the actual last night I had with Owen was when you guys sat in the best seats we have for the Chadwick Boseman dress rehearsal Not the last night. The last snl.*

Leda: *Omg YES exactly. And I was talking w Shanda about it. I'll just send you what I sent her.*

This is what Leda sends me. Her text to her friend Shanda. At first they are talking about Chadwick Boseman.

I know. No wonder he was too tired for a picture . . . I can't believe he took any! But I'll always remember the look on his face when we said how much our students looked up to him. You could tell how much it meant to him - it was his life's purpose. ♥♥♥ (That's part one) And I swear, last night I was all in my feelings and thinking about everyone Owen is getting to meet up there. I literally played out the whole situation where owen obviously wouldn't recognize him at first (classic). Then he'd say "oh, snap!" or something similar and start to text me about it. And I really laughed out loud picturing it as I was brushing my teeth. And just then bathroom lights started flickering. Not like a subtle flicker, like . . . all the way dim, all the way bright. Maybe three times and then all was normal. Can't make this stuff up.

I smile and write back: *And you know my bathroom lightbulb popped.*

Leda: *I know. So I had to tell you.*

Me: *I'm glad you did :) And I remember when that happened it made me laugh because I was thinking "this is great, Owen, but can our place not be the bathroom?"*

I imagine this makes Leda laugh to read. And then I text: *That is really perfect. It's also funny that in you texting me, it reminded me, and then I texted everyone and your dad was also writing about it at the exact same time. So there must have been a moment of Owen right then.*

So I have to explain what I mean there in that last text. After Leda texted, I decided to reach out to the Owen's Angels group text.

Cecily: I just realized that Owen and Leda were in VIP seats at the Chadwick Boseman *SNL* dress rehearsal. We did the earlier show and not the live one (although Leda and Shanda did my dressing room for the air show) because I think Owen had recently started treatments. It was April 7. Leda set it all up ♥

Dr. Henry: So many overlapping circles in our lives ♥♥♥

Me: It was a night of superheroes

Dr. Henry: Absolutely!!! ♥♥

Then Uncle Ed chimes in. He's never as chatty as everyone so I want to see what he says.

Uncle Ed: I was just doing my daily mail to Owen reporting the sad news about Chadwick Boseman when your text arrived. What a convergence of impulses; thank you wonderful Cecily for remembering what must have been a special night for Owen and Leda!

Me: And for me!

And then Laurel writes next, after a couple of minutes.

Aunt Laurel: *Cecily and Leda, thank you so much for making that happen. Knowing that Owen had these special events and times to carry with him gives a certain degree of what. Hope?*

And of course Dr. Henry: *Hope indeed!* ♥♥♥

All of us thinking about Owen in different places at the same time. I imagine him flying with his birds past our homes this morning, at exactly the same moment. So we'd want to reach out to each other. And when we did, we'd feel like maybe he set this up for us. As a way to say hello? A way to make sure we are taking care of each other on a tough day? Owen in flight.

There were beautiful articles written today about what Chadwick Boseman accomplished, and with so much grace, all while being treated for cancer. I'm totally blown away by this person I barely spoke to that week.

So, the world is without two superheroes. I don't know comic books well. So I don't know where that leaves us in comic book land. But for me, as hard as it is, I will leave it here: I think it's great we got to be living here on earth at the same time as two superheroes.

Wakanda Forever.

SEPTEMBER 3, 2020

Jack reached out earlier this week, upset, because a family friend had some bad cancer updates. I guess that's what you call those. I remind him that we can't and don't count people out. That it's a cruel disease but that means it surprises us in both ways. And does your friend want to be treated like she's sick? No. Then don't treat her that way. He says thank you for the reminder. He sees the friend the following day and it's good, normal. The most comforting word. For both of them. He even later reaches out to Dr. Henry, and Dr. Henry makes some calls to fast-track her and get her set up with a good doctor at Sloan Kettering. He does it, he reminds us, because we are a team, a family. It seems to be the only way to take on a supervillain like cancer.

SEPTEMBER 8, 2020

Jack sits next to me on my Airbnb porch, while we soak up the last bits of sun and last bits of summer and last bits of being together before I leave for nine weeks to work.

I'm traveling to Vancouver to film a show I was supposed to have filmed over the summer. I love the show. I love the script. It's a musical comedy and the characters are great and it's full of joy and love and it makes me cry happy tears at every table read we've done. It doesn't even feel real that I get to do it. It's one of those projects that will never feel real, I think, even after it's totally done and someone is watching it across the world. But I'm still terrified. I've said no to this total dream job at least twice. Somehow I've been lucky enough that the people in charge were gentle enough with me—and persistent!—and worked with me to get me to terms and conditions that made me finally feel safe enough to say yes. It really is bizarre, because it's this absolute dream job I've been so excited about for two years, but at the same time I'm crossing a closed border during a pandemic. Nobody can visit me. I can't leave. I have to quarantine again for two weeks. What if something happens to my family while I'm gone? Or me? I'm going to be singing and dancing and kissing, and we can't wear masks while we film, right? I have a lot of anxiety, so I try not to think about it too much. Just remind myself how lucky I am to have the opportunity. Hold on to that.

And hold on to Jack now. I'm gonna miss him.

We've been holding hands a lot, hugging. He's on his zero-gravity chair next to mine. He's texting a friend from college. About fishing or baseball, who knows. And he says to me, "You know, he had cancer and it went away. But I guess it came back in February and he did treatments."

I turn to him. "How is he doing now?"

"I don't know," he says. "I ask him how he's doing, but . . ."

It seems none of us know quite how to talk with each other about cancer.

"It's tough, I know," I say. "You don't want to seem invasive or bring up a thing he doesn't want to be reminded of. But you aren't asking because you want to know how sick he is to decide your manner of speaking to him. You are asking because he's a friend that you care about. I bet you could say something like, 'Hey, I hope you are finished with those treatments. How are you feeling?'"

Jack texts his friend. He responds right away.

"He says he's only got a couple treatments left. But he says he's good. Seems to be responding to treatment."

The response is clipped, but to me that sounds like good news on the horrible warped scale of good and bad when it comes to cancer news. They return to texting about baseball/fishing.

I turn away, look up at the trees who have let me hide all summer. I let myself cry a little. It seems like none of us quite know how to talk about cancer, but it looks like more and more of us are going to have to do it. Then I let myself smile a little, too. I'm happy to hear his friend is okay. I'm happy he asked.

Maybe it's like what Aunt Laurel said and it gives me a little, what. Hope?

SEPTEMBER 13, 2020

Jack Jack you are something else
You called me dandelion,
I call you sunshine
Summer creatures barreling into fall
I pretend I won't wait for you
I won't work for you
But of course I will
I believe in you
And you say I see you?
Well you hear me
You can even read my silent language
You hear what I need
And what a gift to get from someone

Today I was so happy I screamed your name on top of every mountaintop in my home: my kitchen island, my shower, my strange aboveground potted garden.

I ran down my long driveway with the heavy trash cans and I laughed so much with Kevin, because of our crazy awkward movements—heel-toe-heel-toe . . . sort of . . . somehow—and because we were going so outrageously fast.

I feel okay to go now, across the border.

I feel okay about this show.

I never feel okay.

I'm scared of so so so so so so so much.

I never feel this okay.

And now I do.

I've never been able to believe in a handhold, a hug. No matter how otherworldly it felt. No matter how absolutely real I knew it to be.

And now I get to believe in you.

(And my therapist would love to pause right here in this moment to show me that, look, it is possible to feel that connection again. Now resume.)

I'm too special for most of the world.

(I use the word *special* on my best days.)

But then there is you.

With your awkward hugs like being captured.

With your falling asleep after ten minutes on the couch.

With your phone calls and your motorcycle and your good vibes and your trout fishing and your loud-to-louder car. With your winks and your smiles, me never knowing if there is a phone call happening on those things in your ears. Your attention is often elsewhere no matter where we are.

Me with my Ketel botanicals and bad TV and good British TV and anxiety and fears I can laugh at while still knowing they are there. Me with no lights off in the room because I'm most scared of myself in the dark. Me with stubborn beliefs and fears that I think have kept me safe and a propensity to self-sabotage because sometimes I'm so much better at a really fucking good retort than a really fucking good response. I like to throw dynamite and say, "It doesn't fucking matter."

And then you.

And then there is you there.

And you said I lasted three "of these."

Of these moments.

I assume you mean times where I really was drawing a line, ready to walk.

But I'd last ten more.

Because the one keeping track was you, not me, as upset as I seem.

You reach for my hand as much as I reach for yours.

You reach for my hand as much as I reach for yours.

You reach for my hand as much as I reach for yours.

Sorry, I don't get to say that often.

Have I ever?

OCTOBER 13, 2020

"You've done so well in 2020."

I hear it a lot. I've said it, I think. I laugh. I stayed healthy! I got a Netflix animated series! I ended up in a love story! I am filming a new delightful show in Vancouver, where I'm the star and it makes me wonder every day if it's real, if I'm the one who is supposed to look pretty today. Every day. I got a nomination. I've done so well in 2020.

I write that as a joke, because how can I say that? I lost the most beautiful boy. I thought I'd lose another. I worry still that I may. I'm worried I'd lose myself in some way. I lost Hal. My friend lost his grandma. I lost my landlord. Life stopped. But I did well, still, I think. Even if work means wearing thick masks with tests three times a week, separated across a border from my family because nothing is safe. But I'm working. It's good. It's inexplicably good. It makes friends sigh happily to ponder it. And then I go to bed like this, in a beautiful West Vancouver house, looking over water, and I sob. Because maybe I have found ways to share you. Maybe I have felt you around. Maybe it feels like you have a hand in the good news. But there is no changing you are gone. I miss you so much. And I hate GBM.

But just like every dark night, I look up at whatever star formation is there—tonight is too cloudy to see—and I look for you. And if there's nothing, no stars, I look at our skies and I say out loud, "I promise you I want to be better." How much I fucking miss you. I am good at keeping my head up. I want to smile when people say I'm doing well. As well as I can do in October. I lost you in January. I lost you. I love you, Owen.

DECEMBER 3, 2020

There are anniversaries coming up in this story. Some pretty big ones.

Lucy needs a tooth cleaning. I know that because she got her teeth cleaned the day of the Christmas party where I met Jack. The last Thursday in December before *SNL*'s hiatus, right before Jack would go to Cuba. Owen wasn't responding to our group texts in December, but Leda was. So it didn't stick out as much. COVID was apparently in California—where I was, with Rashida. I haven't seen her in ten months. What's a life become when you take so many people out of it?

I am back in New York, in my apartment tonight. It's the second night I've spent at home since March 24, 2020. I almost wrote 2012. That's weird.

Yesterday I got back to my apartment and looked around. There's not much to look at; it's a small space. But I tried to enter the rooms like I didn't want to disturb anything or even really touch anything. At first, I sat on my couch like I always do. I've lived here nine years. Why am I thrown by nine months? I watch TV here. I sit here every Wednesday and lose my mind over the sketches picked for *SNL* and I feel anxious until

I take my herbal sleeping pills and ZzzQuil to sleep. Though since about the beginning of the pandemic, I've become an Ambien gal.

I was doing fine, emotionally I guess, until I looked at the coffee table. Sorry, *my* coffee table. It's mine, isn't it? I have to remind myself these things in this apartment are mine. It's covered in a lot: various weird cosmetic products, like masks and serums and gel nail polishes; sunglasses; cords; pads of cute dog-print stationery; Bluetooth speakers. There are two unopened DNA tests I never took. A book of Rilke my friend got for me when I did my first Second City job, working on a cruise ship for four months.

I was twenty-six and it was my first real paying gig in comedy. I spent four months on the *Norwegian Jewel*, going back and forth between New York, Florida, and Nassau. For the first two months I felt like I was on the best vacation ever. Then by the third month it weirdly started to feel less like vacation and more like purgatory. I missed spending a night on land. I slept on a thin mattress on the floor because they wouldn't give my roommate and me two beds, only one. ("The room is only berthed for one." Bless them.) I went in thinking I'd work out and write and see the world and eat well, when in reality I drank a lot of very cheap wine most nights and gained a bunch of weight. I didn't quite see the world as much as spend every Tuesday drinking giant sugary $2 margaritas at a chain restaurant called Dogs in Port Canaveral, Florida. But it was still my first job! I was now a working comedian! And it inspired the cruise passenger character I used at my *SNL* audition. My apartment in New York isn't far from where the ship docks in New York, so I pass by it pretty often. I like to think it keeps me humble.

I had taken the Rilke off the bookshelf at some point earlier that year, looking at it desperately during one of the moments after your heart has been broken a little and so you think, *POETRY! ANY POETRY!* And the task of finding the perfect poem to totally describe this pain I'm feeling winds up distracting me from this pain I'm feeling.

In front of everything, though, there are four things that hit me hard. It's like they are on display, downstage center. There's the wrapped present I was supposed to give to Leda. It's a framed print of a bird drawing my friends Crystal and Graham made for us after we lost Owen. It's in a square box, wrapped in paper that looks like extensions of the feathers from the wings of the bird in the drawing. Owen's bird.

Next to that wrapped drawing is the COVID care package the young Broadway phenom Syd, Dr. Henry's friend whom I was supposed to mentor, and her mom, Keri, dropped off back in March. The individually wrapped roll of toilet paper. The half-opened box of liposomal vitamin C. I'd only gone through a few packets before I left for the Hudson Valley. Thinking about the generosity of Syd and Keri makes me emotional—their willingness to help out me and Jack when they'd never even met us, and possibly put their own health in jeopardy to do so.

But then I am hit hardest looking at a card lying on the box of vitamin C. I recognize it once I start reading. I was taking notes on whatever I could grab. My handwriting is neat-ish but all over the page, going in different directions. I didn't know what I was writing and so I didn't know what things belonged in the margins and what belonged in the center. Jack was sick and I was asking Dr. Henry what we could do and could we fix this please please please. I wrote useless things that you write because you need to feel like you're not useless: "Sunday let's talk. Monday he can test." "Chills. Keep taking temp." I have a log-in name and password for Jack's doctor's office to get his test results from the flu and strep tests he was allowed to take. So I could let him know and he didn't have to stay looking at the computer. He had that fever.

Up in the right corner I wrote, "Lynn Ratner." Lynn Ratner is the wonderful doctor who agreed to give Jack a COVID test on Monday, March 18. He is in his eighties and quarantined for two weeks after testing Jack. He knew Jack was sick. And underneath Lynn's name, I just wrote, "Owen," and drew a heart around it.

I think I should test out my shower. It feels a little gross in there. I throw out a lot of the product that was in there. Not all. Never all. I turn on the faucet and watch brown gross water coat the tub for twenty seconds. Same thing happens with the shower.

It's not comfortable here. It used to feel comfortable.

I went to bed trying not to touch my sheets. I woke up today and did all the laundry I could. My sheets are clean at least tonight. I had time at home because all my work meetings were over Zoom. I had to leave once to take a lab test for COVID. I'm tested every day.

This apartment has become a natural history museum of me, for me. My life was always messy, but I didn't know what was coming. I didn't know I'd leave in a state of panic and grief and not come back until I'd had a summer in the woods with Kevin and Lucy and Jack. And not until I ran away and made a joyful, magic show in Vancouver for nine weeks.

This girl who was here before me didn't know about everything that would happen. Which is actually maybe normal to say about life any time you look back over a year in which a lot happened. But I think rarely do we have times that feel like this—such a drastic and fast separation, and it lasted nine months. Like being sucked into outer space.

So now, we are getting reacquainted.

Yesterday I finished my first day back at work and only had to take one half of a Xanax. I asked a million questions. "Am I allowed to go to my office? Where do I get that test? Can I order food? Where can I eat? Is it okay to drink water in public? Are all these masks okay to wear? Are any friends okay to hug?" I left that night, headed out to find my car, wearing my mask and gloves. I had to find my car because they can't park at the doors anymore when the tree at Rockefeller Plaza goes up. I hate that tree this year. It makes me feel so unnecessarily endangered. It makes me angry at New York, because aren't we supposed to be doing this well?

Then I started to feel a little warm, because I remembered leaving on a Friday just like this last December. I was looking for my car. When I finally got in I would text Jack, who had left my apartment that morning. He was still in his suit from the party, he said. He was at another Christmas party that night. He ordered a fruit and cheese plate with his friends. He sent me a picture. I liked the picture he sent. Handsome Jack.

Today I think of that again as I run in and out of work to take a lab COVID test—we do rapid tests the other days—and get back into my car to go home to do all my Zoom meetings. I'm learning the routes I'm supposed to take in the building so that we separate as best as possible. I'm trying to be really good at following the rules.

My doorman John gets on the elevator with me at my building. He asks me if I mind. They say only one person or family to an elevator. I say it's okay. We chitchat back and forth before he says that he wants to crunch numbers because he wants to be out of this job, this place, in January. He can't do it anymore. I nod. I don't know how tough that is for him to say. I say something dumb, even though it's still something that I mean: "And nothing has to be a permanent decision. It's not final. You might even start to like doing something else and now you'll give yourself the time."

He smiles and says, "Yeah. Who knows what I may start getting into."

It doesn't feel good, but it doesn't feel awful. Maybe there's something good to take from that. Because we still have to. We still have to look for those things. We really do. Especially now that it seems like we stopped respecting our own grief and pain and even pandemic.

The next day as I leave for work, a woman allows me on the elevator with her. She says, "This is scary." I realize I must look like I'm scared too, in my hood and coat and mask and whatever my pupils have become. I say, "It's my first time back here. I'm only here for work. I'm upstate half the week."

I don't know why I even responded this way.

She says "What? I can't hear with these things."

I smile, as if she can see, and I say, "Yeah, it's the same for me. I can't hear anyone these days."

I don't know what to say next. The elevator stops, and I walk briskly out of the building and to my car.

I didn't know my museum would make me sad. But it does. I think it must be really hard to clean up all of somebody's things when you lose them. The stuff. *Why does she have toilet paper on her table? What's this open box of vitamin C? What are these notes she scratched? I don't know what they mean.*

I told you the notes were written on a card. I turn the card over. Of course. It's a card from a bouquet Leda sent me. She's good, really good, at sending flowers. I think it's from a basketball game I took her to early this year. The night they had the photo of Kobe Bryant up on the wall at MSG because we'd all just found out he was gone. The night Leda and I held hands and cried and cheered, "OW-EN! OW-EN!" while the crowd yelled "KO-BE! KO-BE!" (Again, because we thought Kobe wouldn't mind.) She sent me flowers after that. "Cecily THANK YOU Cec. I love you and I've looked up to your kindness and compassion my whole life—still trying to walk like you. Love, Leda."

And maybe my museum isn't only messy and sad.

JANUARY 7, 2021

It's been a year since you left us, Owen. When I think about the year, it's hard to say what I've learned. Why is that my instinct anyway, in being able to process the passing of time? I guess it makes me feel like time is still linear and the math is linear, in that this much time has passed so that means I must have learned x. But I don't know what I've learned or what I know. Because it feels too much like trying to say there is a lesson in this, and one for which we had to trade you. Nobody would ever do that. That isn't a fair trade.

But I can say there are plenty of things I didn't know prior to last January. Here are some things I didn't know:

I didn't know I'd be living with Kevin in a house in the Hudson Valley.

I didn't know I'd find love a third time. I didn't know if it was something I even needed. I didn't know if it was something I was capable of having—or rather if I was capable of being a good partner to somebody. I didn't know I'd ever feel comfortable with another person in that position in my life, or if instead I'd start to resent them being there. I didn't know it would be possible for me to feel safe with another person.

I didn't know I could feel like someone wouldn't leave me.

I didn't know I could grow cucumbers. Or tomatoes or lettuce or parsley or dill or oregano or basil.

I didn't know how much I liked calla lilies and that I could grow those, too. I didn't and still don't quite know how to plant bulbs. I didn't know a whole lot of sunlight would make up for not knowing anything about seeds and bulbs and soils and fertilizers.

I didn't know deer scream. And they eat the bulbs you plant.

I didn't know how to cook a tofu stir-fry. Or that I'd like it so much.

And going back even farther, I didn't know how big a part of my life my little cousins would become. I didn't know how much I'd love having you and Leda around, and how good it would feel when I'd see my skinny little cousins showing up at going-away parties and birthday parties and basketball games. I didn't know how much I'd enjoy showing you both off: yeah, those two amazing and kind and superintelligent and fun-to-be-around humans are actually my little cousins.

And I didn't know I'd actually lose you. Even after hearing the worst of the worst news that was scary to even say out loud: GBM. You had brain cancer. I still didn't think we'd lose you.

I didn't know how much of a guide you'd become in my life. My younger cousin. I knew you were special, and more courageous than anyone I knew, but I didn't know how much of an impact that part of you would have on my own life after you'd left.

I don't know where you are.

I don't know how long any of us have, or how to ever accept that.

I wish you were here. I know you are not. And that's really the only math I know for sure. It's been a year, Owen. I miss you and I love you.

FEBRUARY 27, 2021

I've been struggling a bit with work. It still scares me to be in the city, living in my apartment building for half of the week. I'm splitting time between the city and the Hudson Valley. It's a bit of a commute, but worth it for the three days I get to live in my beloved woods, not thinking about where I've left my mask. We are double masking these days.

The reason I'm struggling is because I feel the sadness and gloom that have set in around me. I think being back here has made me see and feel what we don't have anymore. We are trying to do a job that is by nature a collaborative process but in a time where collaboration is difficult and always watched over by a team of people in reflective jackets who look for when someone isn't wearing a face shield over their mask correctly or when we start to forget the rules and stand too close to one another. It's their job, and I'm actually fully grateful because they are doing all of this for us. To keep us safe from the virus still raging.

But it's hard to see these people I love so much and not be able to do something as simple as watch a dumb YouTube video together over a phone. We aren't allowed to stand close unless we are rehearsing a scene on set. I don't see anybody's face unless I'm in a sketch with them. And even then, the most I will see anyone's face in person is twice on Saturday: once at dress rehearsal and once at air. I don't enjoy writing as much because we have to do it over Zoom. You can't really banter over Zoom. It's stilted and awkward and there's a camera on your face. Everything feels less funny. The audience is significantly smaller, so performing is much harder. Everything I do feels like I'm bombing. And let me tell you, there is a particular sting in bombing at sketch comedy. I can't help but feel exceptionally pathetic: making a fool of yourself without the validation of laughter. Yeesh.

It's not all bleak, though. We are so fortunate to have jobs right now. And jobs where there is a team of people working hard to keep us safe. And the vaccines are here, with more coming. My dad just got his second dose. I feel hopeful.

I was feeling really low this past Saturday. It was our fifth show in a row. So we were tired. Exhausted. I don't sleep well during show weeks under any circumstances, forget COVID. I'm anxious all week. I'm worried about the live show. Do I have enough in the show? Too much? Am I going to be able to nail this bit in the one chance I have to do it live in front of millions of people? We only get about two real rehearsals. The show is fast and we have to be able to make changes up to sometimes the moment we are physically performing a sketch—seeing writers frantically changing the cue cards five cards ahead of where we are. I'm jittery even writing all of this now.

I played Governor Whitmer again for the first time since the *SNL at Home*. It was written as a piece of the cold open and the sketch is about the vaccine rollout. I don't really care what it's about, though. I know there's only one thing I'm thinking about.

It's just one quick shot, so I try to hold the bottle so the bright orange and blue label can be seen clearly as I take a gulp. A Bell's Oberon. The same beer the governor sent to me at Megan's Airbnb in May.

I'm getting the beer right this time.

I didn't know there would be a "this time," a "next time."

But here I am.

Here we are.

After the show something really special happened. A couple of us stayed around for the first time. It wasn't a big group. I can't really even use the term *party*. We were listening to music and dancing and chatting, even if we were still double masked and physically distanced.

I am standing in the back of the room alone for a moment just watching my friends. I realize I haven't done anything at all like this in about a year. And I miss this *so* much. I love them *so* much. We are going to be able to have this for real again soon. How lucky to even have this night together.

And before I leave, a girl with long dark hair and a mask approaches me. As I realize who it is, I start to tear up.

It's Remi. The girl from work I barely knew who I spoke with over the phone while her mom was hospitalized with COVID. I haven't seen her in person since then.

We break a COVID rule and hug each other because we need to finally hug each other. We've needed this hug for almost a year.

She starts to thank me and wants to tell me how much it meant to her to speak with me while her mom was sick, and I tell her, "No no no, thank you, it meant so much to me to be able to feel helpful in any way." We are spilling these words out even though we really don't even have to say anything at all. Because we know. Of course we know. We went through this scary thing together. During those early days where you knew so little about COVID, you might end up on the phone with a coworker you barely knew because there was really nobody else to ask to give you any kind of information on this virus attacking people we loved.

Almost a year after COVID shut down the world, I'm hugging Remi in a room with my friends and coworkers dancing and laughing around me. We just did a show together. Jack is better. Remi's mom is better. We are all still here.

We are lucky.

I am lucky.

MARCH 1, 2021

What's the ending? I asked when I started writing this. *Would you even know?*

I'm at a Knicks game. Bulls vs. Knicks. I'm with Owen and Leda and my friend and *SNL* castmate Michael Che. The photographer gets photos of us crazy cheering. Owen's got his fists in front of his face and I've got one raised in the air and my mouth is wide open. Leda is doing the same. We are crazed. We are family. I don't remember if they won or lost. We go out afterward and get a drink at an Irish bar. We laugh at Michael ordering bangers and mash. Owen orders a beer. We are laughing. It's a normal night. I like seeing him like this. It makes me think he's gonna be okay. I know he's gonna be okay.

It's the last night I will see Owen.

But I don't want to end that way. I don't like that ending for any story.

In real life I don't have an ending. Or know it. Or believe there even is one, or if there is, then *only* one. I'm still very much in the middle. Or somewhere. Maybe the beginning of a new world. Maybe the end of an old life. I honestly don't know. I'm somewhere in time and space.

It does seem likely, though, everything will

have changed permanently. Some people seem to think that implies a negative change. I think I used to be a person like that. Maybe part of me still is. But then there's a part of me that wants to be more open now, to allowing love to grow, even in times of grief and fear. I'm trying to get comfortable with living with the unknown day to day, just as my hero did for almost two years.

Here's a thing I know for sure: I had a cousin named Owen who had red hair as a little boy and he was a serious kid and he loved birds. He taught me about love during his life and he's teaching me about love after.

"Do as It May" by the Evening Fools

And while I know
The days may be unfriendly to me soon
If even every shoulder turn cold,
  I know I can turn to you
And you will shine, baby
A beacon on a tower 'cross the sea
Leading me through treacherous tides
Stronger than you could believe
If even all sounds comin' 'cross my ears
  are screamin'
I don't have to hear them just with
  one whisper from you, babe
And every time you tell me it's all right
  ain't nothing that I can't survive
As I meet my troubles day to day
Long as I got you, girl
Let the world do as it may
Long as I got you, girl
Let the world do as it may
And even though
Mountains need a-movin' every day
From the air she conjures the time
  for her darlin' all the same
And while I try, baby
To make myself be worthy of her heart

Every time her kindness unfolds
Sends me right back to the start

And what does one do
To deserve being lucky as I?
What gracious star has fallen
For this to be true
Or is her love a generous lie?
But I don't need the answer 'cause

Long as I got you, girl
Let the world do as it may

ACKNOWLEDGMENTS

First of all, I want to thank my amazing editor, Sean, at Simon & Schuster. From the day I heard my literary agents almost yelp with excitement while saying your name, I knew I was working with a rock star. Not only would this book not have happened in general without you, I can think of about fifteen days just off the top my head that I would have probably thrown my hands up in the air and given up without you talking me off a ledge in some way or another. Thank you for holding my hand through all of it and making me cry at every detailed and thoughtful email response to the writing I sent you. I'm so happy and so lucky you are part of my story.

For Cindy, Cait, Josh, and Rachel at CAA; and Tim at Brillstein—your encouragement and support mean more to me than you know. Thank you for telling me to keep writing early on after I, without explanation, sent you a random essay last year. Thank you for sharing your own stories. And thank you for persuading me to do something kind of insane by writing this book!

Thanks to Lauren Roseman, Lauren Manasevit, Kate Childs, and the wonderful S&S marketing/publicity duo of Maggie Southard and Elizabeth Breeden for knowing not only what this book is, but how to get it out to the right places. Thanks for taking this on and helping me share my cousin.

For Lorne—well for starters, thank you for changing my life ten years ago. And for all the times you've changed my life since then. And thank you for reminding me that it's okay to show your heart AND do comedy. Who knew?

For Rashida, my little sis—thank you for trusting me. Thank you for inspiring me and teaching me but most importantly making me laugh so damn much. Thank you for bringing Queen Sabrina into my life! I love you, sis.

For Jack—thank you for driving me crazy in all the good and bad ways. Thank you for letting me share so much of our story. And thank you for all the things I get to keep to myself. You were, and every day continue to be, such a wonderful surprise to me.

For Kevin, Joel, Matt, Graham, Crystal, Erin, Tommy, Shawn, Markus, Bianca, Sam, Cayenne, Laura, Susannah, and Caitlin—thank you for being my chosen family. I love you all so much.

For Mama, Dad, Nat, Colleen, Sammi, Steve, Sarah, Josh, and Jack—thank you for being my bio and "non-bio" family. I love you all and can't wait to finally see you all again! And Mama—thank you for being the person I knew would read the book as soon as I sent it. This book is for your B and H, too.

For Ed, Laurel, and Leda—thank you for taking such great care of me, kind of immediately and no questions asked, in New York. You're all really good at this "family" thing.

And for Owen, Liz, Erica, Hal, Monét—thank you for all the ways you made life so much more beautiful, funny, colorful, magical, musical, and wonderful for all the people who share the giant gift and devastation of missing you very much. Aren't we all lucky to have gotten to share our own time on this earth with you.

Books are
produced in the
United States
using U.S.-based
materials

Books are printed
using a revolutionary
new process called
THINKtech™ that
lowers energy usage
by 70% and increases
overall quality

Books are
durable and
flexible
because of
Smyth-sewing

Paper is
sourced using
environmentally
responsible
foresting methods
and the
paper is acid-free

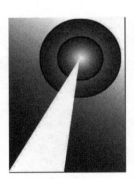

Center Point Large Print
600 Brooks Road / PO Box 1
Thorndike, ME 04986-0001 USA

(207) 568-3717

US & Canada:
1 800 929-9108
www.centerpointlargeprint.com